11167

8.2

P9-CSF-750

Longman St...

Androcles and the Lion

822
SHA.
No.

11167

Longman Study Texts   **General editor: Richard Adams**

Titles in the series:

Androcles and the Lion   11408
SHAW, Bernard
                                822 Sha

Good Counsel College Library

Bernard Shaw

Androcles and the Lion

edited by
Patrick Colton

with a personal essay by
John Russell Brown

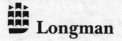
Longman

LONGMAN GROUP LIMITED
Longman House
Burnt Mill, Harlow, Essex, CM20 2JE, England
and Associated Companies throughout the world

Copyright 1913, 1916, 1930, 1941, 1944 George Bernard Shaw
Copyright 1957 The Public Trustee as Executor of
the Estate of George Bernard Shaw

This edition © Longman Group Limited 1986
All rights reserved; no part of this publication
may be reproduced, stored in a retrieval system,
or transmitted in any form or by any means, electronic,
mechanical, photocopying, recording or otherwise,
without the prior written permission of the Publishers.

This edition first published 1986
ISBN 0 582 33091 2

Set in Baskerville 10/12 pt, Linotron 202.

Produced by Longman Group (F.E.) Limited
Printed in Hong Kong

Contents

CONTENTS

We are grateful to Margery Morgan, Reader in English at the University of Lancaster, for her advice and contribution to the Introduction and Notes in this edition.

Margery Morgan is the author of *The Shavian Playground: An Exploration of the Art of G B Shaw* (Methuen 1972), *Pygmalion* and *Major Barbara* in the York Notes series (Longman 1980). She has edited *The Doctor's Dilemma* in the series *Shaw: Early Plays in Facsimile* (Garland Publishing, New York, 1982) as well as writing two pamphlets and many articles on Bernard Shaw.

A personal essay

by John Russell Brown

The plays of Bernard Shaw

I have never known what to say about the plays of Bernard Shaw, and never been quite certain how to study them. I sometimes think that I enjoy them too much.

Perhaps I should begin by stating the obvious. According to the standards of practical and profitable theatre, Bernard Shaw is one of the greatest dramatists in the whole world. At first he experienced difficulty in having his plays performed because of censorship or because he could not get an appropriate theatre or the right cast to perform them. *Widowers' Houses,* which he started to write in 1884, was the earliest to be produced, but it was put on by J T Grein's Independent Theatre Society in 1892 for only two special performances. But now, more than ninety years since he decided to write for the stage and more than thirty since his death in 1950, Bernard Shaw can pack theatres in every English-speaking nation and in many others besides.

He wrote more than fifty plays of varying length, and more than a dozen of them have been renowned successes almost from the first. Their star parts have attracted the very best actors of each generation and have proved responsive to many changes of fashion, thought and social expectations. The passage of time has not rendered them obsolete but discovered new strengths, unexpected comedy and further subtleties of characterization. Shaw's dialogue, especially, has remained immediately accessible – animated, fascinating and apparently new-minted.

Not all the plays we enjoy today were received at first with acclamation. Some press criticisms of *Androcles and the Lion,* after its first production in 1913, are representative in their variance from each other:

A very discursive and ill-knit play, which is, moreover, bound to give offence to not a few...

The Morning Post

A really bright and brilliant piece of work, not half so portentous as Mr Shaw can be when he likes...

The Daily Chronicle

Even while we laughed we had some qualms of conscience...

The Daily Telegraph

Laughter long and loud vollied and even thundered in the St James's Theatre last night. It was not the cynical, ill-natured laughter that often marks a Shaw première, but merriment – glad, spontaneous and uncontrolled...

The Evening Standard

The present play is not even up to the level of *Caesar and Cleopatra*, by no means one of Shaw's best efforts...

The Daily Herald

In later life Shaw used to say that each one of his plays was hailed as a masterpiece, except the last one. He quoted a critic's description of him as 'a dignified monkey shying coconuts at a bewildered public', and professed to be 'touched' at the softening adjective, 'dignified'.

Bernard Shaw did not make it easy for his critics, because he never stopped drawing attention to himself, telling others what to think and cultivating an arresting public *persona* that was somewhat comic and occasionally tiresome. In part this may be due to spending all his early years as an outsider: a naturally curious boy, dissatisfied at school; an Irishman in exile; an unpublished novelist; a bachelor until the age of forty-two. He had come to London from Dublin in 1876 at the age of twenty, having already worked as a land-agent's clerk for more than four years. Now he was joining his mother and sister in order to become a writer, but he earned only a pittance for ten industrious years before gaining recognition. Not until 1887 did the fourth of his novels become the first to be published in book form.

The very titles of these works suggest their writer's long and self-conscious pursuit of success and of his own proper place in life: *Immaturity*, *The Irrational Knot*, *Love Among the Artists*, *Cashel Byron's Profession* (he was a pugilist), *An Unsocial Socialist*. The last of these reflects Shaw's membership of the Fabian Society which dated from 1884 and led to immediate and frequent engagements as a public speaker. In support of this socialist group's determination to 'reconstruct society', he addressed whatever public he could find, on Clapham Common or in small meetings of sympathizers. He gained in exchange a ready turn of clear-sounding phrase, a tone of conviction and a keen sense for the reactions of an audience. All this new experience and new company was valuable to the alert and hard-working writer, and may well have precipitated his movement towards the stage. At about the same time he started to work as a book reviewer and soon afterwards made a name for himself as a weekly music critic and drama critic. When he was thirty-six his first play was produced.

Bernard Shaw was so long in finding his true profession as a dramatist that it seems quite natural that he never lost a youthful zest for this work, retaining into his nineties a love of experiment, fantasy and the unexpected. Almost all his plays raise questions of dramatic propriety that would have been avoided by any ordinarily accomplished writer. Why should an Epilogue bring back the Dauphin some twenty-five years after the end of *Saint Joan*, so that the Maid can appear to him in a 'pallid greenish light' to be followed by various other 'visions'? Why tie up every minute circumstance in *Arms and the Man* and leave so much in the air at the end of *Pygmalion*, especially when every reader of the text is told what happens after the fall of the curtain in an Epilogue? Is it only an extravagant whim – it could not be inexperience or lack of respect for financial problems – that calls for a taxicab to arrive on stage to carry off Eliza Doolittle at the end of Act I of *Pygmalion*? Why demand two elaborate time-consuming changes of the set in the middle of Act I of *Caesar and Cleopatra* so that a short dialogue can take place while the characters are standing between the paws of the sphinx in the middle of the desert?

Mrs Patrick Campbell, the first Eliza in *Pygmalion*, used to call the play's author 'Joey' as if he were a clown; but that, like Shaw's own public fooling, was nowhere near a full indication of the man or of his plays. Other admirers – and himself in certain moods – could see 'GBS' as a prophet, a topical political thinker. (The Prime Minister and Leader of the Opposition came to see a play he wrote about the state of Ireland.) He tackled large and timely issues such as the future of Christianity, the terrors and attractions of war, the possibility of international disarmament and the role of a poet in society. He wrote *Man and Superman* about evolution and the function of what he called 'The Life Force'; and he published this play with an Epistle Dedicatory – and explanatory – together with a *Revolutionist's Handbook and Pocket Companion*. In the five parts of *Back to Methuselah*, Shaw moved the action from 4004 BC through the centuries to 31,920 AD, which he said was 'As Far As Thought Can Reach'. He published a collection of 'Trifles and Tomfooleries', but he also caused the critics to class him with Ibsen as a supreme Dramatist of Ideas.

Indeed Shaw's plays are full of ideas, discussed at considerable length by their characters and affecting the development of those characters and the situations in which they are presented. No one could miss the author's concern with contemporary politics, morality, science, sociology, education, religion, history, philosophy, bureaucracy and sexuality. He went to great lengths to elaborate his notions further in prefaces, statements and free-ranging essays. He used the occasion of publishing a dramatic text to address his readers on 'Parents and Children', on 'Diabolonian Ethics', 'Better Than Shakespear?' and other topics arising in the plays. He is often so opinionated in the statements these prefaces make about the plays that he may mislead the reader. (There is, of course, no preface when the play is staged in a theatre.) A very brief example is this 'explanation' of an early comedy:

In *The Philanderer* I have shewn the grotesque sexual compacts made between men and women under marriage laws which represent to some of us a political necessity (especially for other people), to some a divine ordinance, to some a romantic ideal, to some a domestic profession for women, and to some the worst of blundering abominations, an institution which society has outgrown but not modified, and which 'advanced' individuals are therefore forced to evade.

It can be very inhibiting to actors and directors to read such passages, and to read Shaw's elaborate stage directions, which were not intended for them but to help readers who could not see the play and had to make do with a printed text. Imaginative stage interpretation and careful reading of the plays themselves will often bring out further, and perhaps different meanings not allowed for in Shaw's dogmatic assertions. (I recommend readers to turn to the prefaces only when they are thoroughly familiar with the plays they accompany.) Shaw himself confessed that particular ideas were only a secondary element in a thoroughly good play. When he was asked to contribute to a symposium on 'Should social problems be freely dealt with in the Drama?', he conceded that topical ideas could give an immediate interest to a play, but he went on to stress that they are not necessary. Age, love, death, accident, and 'personal character' all lie outside social institutions, but it is these that give permanent interest to drama, independent of period or place.

In one of his reviews, reprinted in *Our Theatres in the Nineties*, Bernald Shaw wrote that 'people's ideas, however useful they may be for embroidery, especially in passages of comedy, are not the true stuff of drama, which is always the naïve feeling underlying the ideas'.

There is a paradox here which can only be understood by realizing that Shaw's own 'naïve feelings' were dominated by a passionate desire to understand, to be intellectually in control of feeling, laughter, and happiness, as well as argument. He wanted a drama that reflected his own sense of being most alive when in pursuit of some idea or action in which he could have absolute faith. In this he was a resolute romantic, a writer in quest of some secret that was always eluding him. Many of the plays express such an involvement directly:

Everything I think is mocked by everything I do.

Arms and the Man

I think I'm going to die for God. Nothing else is real enough to die for. – What is God? – When we know that, Captain, we shall be gods ourselves.

Androcles and the Lion

What is life but a series of inspired follies? The difficulty is to find them to do.

Pygmalion

I'm always expecting something. I don't know what it is; but life must come to a point sometime.

Heartbreak House

But a single character can never speak wholly for this dramatist: he gave self-confidence and uninhibited clarity to each one of his *dramatis personae* so that the excitement of a play is especially in their *inter*play. Innocence is offset by expediency, personal inspiration by corporate wisdom, deceit by honesty, practicality by vision. The typical ending of Shaw's greatest plays is a moment of balance: sometimes between two people, as in *Man and Superman*; or, more often, between a larger grouping, as in *Heartbreak House, Pygmalion, You Never Can Tell*, and *Candida. Saint Joan* concludes with the words of the Maid alone, but these come at the end of an Epilogue which has surveyed a great stretch of European history; they are, perhaps, the most generalized expression of this romantic sentiment:

> O God that madest this beautiful earth, when will it be ready to receive Thy saints? How long, O Lord, how long?

Underlying the plays, in all their fantasies, jokes, surprises, provocations and serious argumentations, is their author's passionate insecurity, his unfulfilled desire to understand the whole business and absurdity of life around him, to know what it is like to see with each person's eyes and feel with each person's senses and intelligence. But he is not a gloomy romantic and optimism usually shines through. When Shaw shows men killing each other or submitting to injustice or self-denial, the play is never quite at an end: a joke, a shift of time or a change of focus alters any situation he is able to imagine. He draws audiences into theatres because he shares the exhilaration of his own endless passion to understand.

I have referred frequently to audiences and theatres with good reason. On the page, the plays of Bernard Shaw cannot easily exert their full fascination and this is the prime difficulty of studying them. His writing is so lucid and his vocabulary so simple that it is easy to avoid reading him as attentively as he deserves. His contemporaries, Henry James and W B Yeats, and many other authors a good deal younger than himself, such as D H Lawrence, James Joyce, T S Eliot or Virginia Woolf, wrote in styles that are very obviously of great complexity, depth, originality and subtlety, and they put readers at once upon their mettle and challenge comprehension. In contrast, the style of 'GBS' is un-poetic, and his most brilliant passages are perfectly comprehensible. (The public speaker and the journalist are evident here.) The first step towards a proper appreciation of Shaw is to realize that all his dialogue is designed to be understood as part of the actors' performances. Its subtlety and depth are revealed only in action, infused with feeling and individual reality as the whole play comes to life. Shaw's style could be described as music written for several carefully contrasted instruments, each with its individual tone and requiring an individual instrumentalist.

This does not mean that actors can appreciate readily what comes to a reader only with difficulty. Shaw was quick to agree that his plays needed very special acting and that great virtuosity was required for their 'sudden transitions of mood'. He told a director that his chief task would be to prevent actors taking their tone and speed from one another and 'thus destroying the continual variety and contrast which are the soul of liveliness in comedy and truth in tragedy'. He saw his works as traditional but, at the same time, out-of-fashion because they required larger-than-life performance. He called for a response to his texts similar to that given to Italian and German opera:

> I went back to the classical style and wrote long rhetorical speeches like operatic solos, regarding my plays as musical performances precisely as Shakespear did.

He was 'furiously opposed' to Pinero, Henry Arthur Jones, and other contemporary playwrights who sought realistic speech for their characters: in his view, they pretended to present a picture of life on stage, but placed nothing there but a collection of 'clockwork mice' and 'chemical rabbits'.

Any student of Shaw's plays should try to see them acted by the very best performers when they have got the full measure of their parts. (Actors find that rehearsals of Shaw are very difficult indeed, until they catch the right sound or tempo or pitch to release the truth and vitality of their roles.) In default of that, we should try to imagine the lively interplay of a play's speeches and actions, not read them through silently at a great pace, enjoying simply the art of a master storyteller and stopping only for the very few words that we may not fully understand. Reading a whole play aloud will not be very much help either, although Shaw used to start rehearsals by doing just that himself for his cast. The strong dynamics of the writing must be appreciated. To achieve that it is better to spend a lot of time in reading just one introductory or lively scene and then re-reading it again and again, at first slowly and then more quickly, but always attempting as strong a contrast as possible in speed, tone, manner *and* pitch, between each and every speech. Then it should be possible to introduce transitions within some of the individual speeches, until the whole scene strikes hard and clear with the shafts of Shaw's invention – and ricochets with their splinters. A more difficult, but equally necessary task would be to take one of the long 'arias' and mark that out with a comparable vocal variety and vivacity. Such experiments need a great deal of mental energy and may lead to wild and whirling words, as well as some loss of sense; but the basic qualities of Shaw's dramatic style are almost sure to be discovered in the process.

Of course more than fireworks are needed to bring the plays alive in our imaginations. A commitment must be given to each character in each scene, every moment he or she is on stage: only then will a full flowering occur. Laurence Olivier found the character of Sergius in *Arms and the Man* a 'stupid, idiot part', difficult and thankless to perform. But then, after a performance, the director Tyrone Guthrie said to him 'But don't you love Sergius?' From that moment Olivier no longer thought that he had simply to conform, to provide the cues for Shaw's ideas: '... it clicked, and something happened, I suppose, that gave me a new attitude ... that had been completely lacking in me'. (from *Great Acting*, BBC, edited by H Burton). Shaw's letters to the actors and actresses who played his major roles – Mrs Patrick Campbell, Ellen Terry, George Alexander, Louis Calvert and Sybil Thorndike are only a few of the more famous – all show a concern to get things 'right' and to engage the imagination of the performers fully. His disappointments were expressed with equal vehemence: when *Major Barbara* was running at the Court Theatre, London, he sent a message to Charles Wyndham and Mary Moore in New York:

> I am afraid I shall have to withdraw it unless you both come
> and play for me, for nothing else can save that terrible last
> act. It can be done but we have not got anywhere near it yet.
> (from *All on Stage* by Wendy Trewin, Harrap)

When a whole cast responds to Shaw's musical, muscular writing, when the rhetorical and argumentative points are made clearly, firmly and lightly, when jokes, feelings, thoughts and fantasies are played with complete belief and every role is given its utmost individual worth, then these plays exhilarate and delight. To appreciate them as we read, we must try to imagine all that: and Shaw's writing is so devised that we shall find the adventure is easier than it sounds, and gets easier and more irresistible with practice. In the process we shall find that there is so much we want to say about the plays of Bernard Shaw that it is hard to know where to begin.

Introduction

It's a lively and mischievous imagination that contrives a plot in which the Christian martyrs are thrown to a pantomime lion – a noble beast this one, not only can he express affection and show understanding, he can also dance an excellent waltz! – and tells the story of the Roman persecution of Christians with a wicked mixture of comedy, farce, and deadly seriousness. And it's a brave man who presents such a vision, as Shaw did at the St James's Theatre, London, in September 1913, to the British middle class of the time. Nowadays, a performance of *Androcles and the Lion* is a guaranteed popular success, understandably so, for it is an extremely funny play, recognized as one of Shaw's most amusing and entertaining works. It is also a very interesting example of Shaw's blending comedy and fantasy into extravaganza to make a strong moral point. However, as with many original works, before and since, the first production met with little public or critical approval. Although people as varied in their beliefs as the atheist H G Wells and the Roman Catholic G K Chesterton found the play to be an accurate, witty, representation of Christianity, the first night was greeted by parts of the audience with hissing and booing. Critics, with few exceptions, condemned what they chose to see as a mockery of Christianity and an insult to Christian feelings. After a short run the play was withdrawn. This kind of response was not unusual for a Shaw play. Very few of his works were not at first greeted with howls of disgust and accusations of bad taste. There is little doubt that Shaw was delighted with the moral indignation his fable play caused, and only disappointed that it failed to pay its way.

Shaw and the theatre

At the time of writing *Androcles and the Lion* – just before the First World War, when the German build-up of arms caused the kind of concern that Russian and American build-ups are causing now – Shaw was at the height of his considerable powers: *Pygmalion* (1913) (later turned into the famous musical, *My Fair Lady*) was about to be produced; he had yet to write probably his greatest play, *Heartbreak House* (1917), and the popular *Saint Joan* (1923) for which he won the Nobel Prize for Literature. Nevertheless he already had so many successes behind him – *Arms and the Man* (1894), *Man and Superman* (1903), *John Bull's Other Island* (1904), *Major Barbara* (1905) – that he could be safely recognized as the greatest playwright in the land. Yet, despite this obvious success, success for which Shaw worked extremely hard over a long period of time, the dismissive, outraged criticism that *Androcles and the Lion* received was always with him. There were also several brushes with the Lord Chamberlain's Office, then responsible for theatre censorship. His first play, *Widowers' Houses* (1892), an attack on slum landlords, was performed by a theatre club formed to present new, disturbing plays about real social problems, the kind of material that was likely to be censored or rejected by the popular theatre. In 1896, *Mrs Warren's Profession*, in which Shaw likened the economic system of the country to the running of a brothel, was banned. And in 1911 *The Shewing-up of Blanco Posnet* was banned on the grounds that it would offend *respectable* Christians! One reason why Shaw's plays caused so much adverse criticism is that he often chose serious and contentious subjects and approached them from an unusual point of view. Frequently, as in *Androcles and the Lion*, religion and religious orthodoxy were the central themes around which he spun his artful combination of witty dialogues and farcical events in an attempt to make his audiences think about their society, see it in a new light, and want to change it. Like many revolutionaries before him – and this is one of the important themes in *Androcles and the Lion* – Shaw found himself up against an often cynical authority that preferred things to stay as they were.

Shaw died at his home in Hertfordshire, England, in 1950 at the age of 94. In a career lasting almost sixty years he wrote more than fifty plays, many acknowledged masterpieces, and had been responsible for changing the nature of British theatre from a place of mere entertainment to something at least capable of talking seriously and realistically about the society in which it was placed. In view of his vast output and long career it remains a curious fact that Shaw was almost forty before his first play was produced, and had to wait a further ten years before his sustained success was assured. During that period he wrote a considerable number of plays which, as they were not taken up by the commercial theatre, and as he was determined to get his work before the wider public, he published in book form, accompanying each play with a Preface which discussed the issues raised in the drama. Shaw continued with this method of publication even after his plays were successfully performed. Frequently, however, the Preface was written long after the play, as in the case of *Androcles and the Lion*, and occasionally had little direct relevance to the drama concerned. Yet if the length of the entertaining Preface that accompanies this play, as well as the additional Prefatory Note and Afterword, both written for performances of the play, are anything to go by, then Shaw clearly attached considerable importance to this work and the message it was created to deliver.

Shaw's early life and career

George Bernard Shaw was born in Dublin, Ireland, in 1856, the third child and only son of George and Lucinda Shaw. His father was an unsuccessful corn merchant who had a drinking problem which contributed to the extreme difficulty he had in providing for his wife and children. His mother had a great love of music, something she passed on to her children, and a good singing voice. During Shaw's childhood she trained as a singer and music teacher. Soon after Shaw had completed school she left home with her two daughters, and followed her music teacher, George Lee, to London. There she made a successful career for herself. In 1876, having spent five tedious years as a clerk-cashier in a land agent's office, Shaw too packed his bags and left for London.

The next few years were spent living at his mother's house, generally at her expense, while he sought a suitable career and took on the long process of self education. Shaw had never taken an interest in formal education and had left school a dismal failure. In London he spent many hours in the British Museum Reading Room in pursuit of knowledge and ideas. This unusual and diverse education considerably helped him to develop into the individual and progressive thinker he was later recognized to be. Eventually he decided to become a novelist and between 1879 and 1883 he wrote five novels, only two of which were published at that time: *Cashel Byron's Profession* (1885) and *An Unsocial Socialist* (1886).

Journalism

His books made no money, but in 1886 his luck turned. Through a friend – William Archer, an established journalist – Shaw was appointed art critic to the *World*. Thus began an important phase in Shaw's development. In 1888 he became music critic to the *Star* and in 1895 theatre critic for the *Saturday Review*. This allowed him to earn a small income and to meet many important people in the world of the arts. It also allowed him to give critical support to certain artists he favoured, notably the German composer, Wagner, and the Norwegian playwright, Ibsen, who was then shaking Europe with his radical views. In 1891 Shaw published *The Quintessence of Ibsenism* in which he described Ibsen as a reforming and realistic playwright, one who tackled the problems of modern society and whose dialogue contained genuine discussion of them. He saw Ibsen's objective as that of challenging his audiences by presenting the issues he raised in his plays through the perspective of an unusual moral view, while at the same time attacking middle-class values, conventions, and hypocrisy. It is exactly this approach that we find present in the early Shaw plays.

Socialism

One thing that fired Shaw at this time was social reform. This, together with his connection with the growing socialist movement, was to form the moral basis for his plays, through which he asked his audiences to examine their conduct and characters. In 1884 he joined the influential Fabian Society. Fabians believed in the re-organization of society towards socialism in gradual stages. They believed that social reform should lead to equality and the abolition of poverty, and that these changes were more likely to come from above than from the working class. Throughout his life Shaw dedicated much of his time to the promotion of socialism, not only through his plays, but by writing many books and pamphlets, and even occasionally lecturing on street corners.

Shaw's was, however, a rather unconventional socialism for it was deeply affected by his belief in what he called Creative Evolution. Evolution is a system of ideas about the nature of the world, how it changes and develops. There are, of course, several different explanations as to how evolution takes place and this has been one of the great questions of the nineteenth and twentieth centuries, if not of all time. In Shaw's day the most popular ideas on evolution were those attributed to Charles Darwin (1809–82) and to these Shaw was very much opposed. Darwin's view of evolution was that change in Nature was based on the processes of natural selection and the survival of the fittest. In this view all change in the world is accidental or circumstantial – a mixture of hereditary and environmental factors – and in no way involves the conscious will of the creatures (or vegetation) concerned.

Shaw's principal objections to this view of how change comes about in the world account for his belief in Creative Evolution.

Although he accepts Darwin's explanation as a partial view of how evolution works he also makes it clear that Darwin, in allowing no individual's influence in his version of evolution, has banished the conscious will to make change in the world. As a socialist such a view is unacceptable to Shaw. It is an important part of socialist thought that humankind can consciously change its environment and itself. Shaw preferred to believe that people could consciously will and initiate change in much the same way as a weight-lifter develops muscle to lift weights or ideas are evolved to solve problems. So, for Shaw, Creative Evolution is an affirmation of the individual person's positive, consciously willed involvement in changing his or her nature and that of the world. With the application of clear thinking about his or herself an individual can move from a state of ignorance to one of self understanding, and to positive action in the world based on that understanding. In most of Shaw's plays this is a path taken by at least one character. In *Androcles and the Lion* it is Lavinia who achieves such fulfilment. Creative Evolution was Shaw's spiritual philosophy as well as a basis for socialism. Shaw rejected the concept of an afterlife and a supernatural God, and stressed the importance of this world and this life as the only ones. It follows that we are bound to make the best of them rather than transfer our hopes for a better world in heaven. Socialism, in Shaw's view, is the way to achieve this better world.

Although Shaw claimed to be an atheist, his particular kind of socialism, his strong support for the positive, progressive attitudes to life, and his emphasis of the spiritual side of human nature, marked him out as a very religious man. Certain aspects of his behaviour, for example his championing of spiritual values, his campaigning against vivisection, his vegetarianism, and his refusal to touch alcohol, made him seem more of a Christian than the average person who claims to be one. In fact, in Androcles himself there is much we can recognize as Shaw's own values.

Religion

Shaw had little regard for Christianity or the Church. He rejected the idea, common even today, that Christianity is the one true religion and that non-believers are damned. As Shaw makes clear in his Preface, Christianity is a religion that allows considerable social injustice. Through its doctrine of salvation in the next world it allows all sorts of wrongs to go uncorrected, and shows a considerable contempt for this world and the people in it. This aspect of Christianity is satirized, in the play, by Spintho whose catch-phrase is '. . . all martyrs go to heaven, no matter what they have done' (p. 126). What Shaw demanded of a religion was that it should inspire believers to *make* a better world. Thus religion and politics are closely linked, for mass improvement must necessarily come through the State, progressively altering the structure of society, on positive, humane criteria, towards a greater quality of life for all humankind.

It is often asked why Shaw spent so much time attacking Christianity when its influence and credibility were rapidly shrinking. Many of Shaw's best plays deal directly with religion: *Major Barbara* (the heroine is a member of the Salvation Army) and *Saint Joan* are two obvious examples. A less evident example is *Man and Superman* where Shaw deals directly with his theories on social reform and Creative Evolution. Part of the answer is that Shaw wanted his audience to transfer their commitment from Christianity to socialism as part of a *positive* acceptance of new values. He wanted to take religion back from non-believers and cynics who use it to maintain their power, and he used his art to inspire living religion. Also he was aware that the Church continued to hold considerable influence over people on questions of morality and, equally important, that governments attempt to keep the spiritual out of politics. In *Androcles and the Lion* much of this is apparent. No Roman pays more than lip-service to official religion. The Christians are seen as a nuisance to the state because they do not conform to the official morality and therefore threaten the established order. At this level the Christians in Shaw's Ancient Rome might be seen to be in the same position as the socialists in Shaw's Modern Britain.

Religion and the theatre

The relationship between religion and drama is a close one and the beginnings of Western drama can be traced to the religious festivals of Ancient Greece. In England, during the Middle Ages, when the official religion was Roman Catholic, this relationship took the form of Mystery plays. Many towns performed biblical stories such as Noah's Ark, the Birth of Jesus, the Crucifixion. The actors were amateurs and performances were probably preceded by a church service. Humour was admitted into these plays when suitable, exploiting the strangeness of such situations as when Noah is asked to build his Ark in the middle of a desert, or Joseph's natural disbelief when he is told how Mary became pregnant. Shaw's witty treatment of religion is not without tradition though many of his original audience found it disrespectful.

The religious Reformation shattered the relationship between drama and Church. Protestants thought it blasphemous to dramatize the Bible. In Cromwell's time Puritans succeeded in closing the theatres. Churchmen have often regarded the theatre as an evil place and sought to contain its activities. As late as the 1890s, when Shaw was starting his career as a playwright, it was still illegal to represent the Bible on the stage. In 1893 Oscar Wilde's *Salomé* was banned on these grounds. But in 1896 Wilson Barrett's *The Sign of the Cross* appeared on the London stage and initiated a form of drama known as Christian melodrama. Shaw reviewed the play and clearly did not like it. Yet this play is important to our understanding of *Androcles and the Lion* as Shaw took his plot straight from *The Sign of the Cross* and altered it to make his own points about Christianity.

The structure of Androcles and the Lion

Despite its length – little more than an hour in performance – the play is a complex mixture of several elements. First, as noted above, Shaw has taken the plot of a Christian melodrama – though he has turned it upside down – and a considerable number of its stock scenes and characters. Secondly, he has taken an old fable from Ancient Greece – the story of Androcles and his lion – with which he has surrounded the Christian melodrama, and he presents this familiar tale in the form of a pantomime. There is considerable advantage in examining these two parts separately before considering their overall effect when combined.

1 Christian melodrama and *Androcles and the Lion*

Melodrama is a popular form of entertainment today, just as it was in Shaw's time. Anyone who has seen a Hammer film or a cops and robbers series on television is familiar with this type of story telling. As excitement is the chief objective the characters are usually one-dimensional, not rounded personalities, plots are similar and predictable, and the triumph of hero and heroine seldom in doubt. Also the moral views of the audience are not challenged but are actually confirmed. Generally a melodrama offers the triumph of 'good' over 'evil' through all kinds of awful circumstances. Christian melodrama is similar with regard to characterization and plot but the moral point is that Christian 'good' will always triumph, confirming in the process that Christianity is the only true religion.

Shaw claimed that melodrama was not a representation of 'real life' but of our 'romantic imaginings', adding that drama should have 'the power to imagine things as they really are'. He frequently used melodramatic plots and situations, and occasionally, as here, took plots more or less wholesale from other plays, reworking them to his own design. This, as we have seen, is to challenge the preconceptions of his audience – as they are embodied in the familiar melodrama – with his own ideas. It is not his objective to write a Christian melodrama but to expose the hypocrisy in the content of such dramas.

Plot

The Sign of the Cross avoided the problem of putting biblical events on the stage by presenting the glamorous tale of Mercia, a young, beautiful, Christian woman who is thrown to the lions in Ancient Rome. She has the alternative of marrying Marcus Superbus (!), a Roman Prefect, and saving her mortal life. Their love is central, and eventually it is she who converts him and, hand-in-hand, they both go to their deaths in the arena. This kind of situation will be familiar to anyone who has seen the popular Hollywood epics of the 1950s such as *Ben Hur* and *Quo Vadis?*. Indeed, both these stories were presented as plays on the London stage in the early 1900s in the wake of the success of *The Sign of the Cross*. It is worth emphasizing that so similar are all Christian melodramas that Shaw's parody – and criticism – is applicable to the entire genre.

In *Androcles and the Lion* the Captain and Lavinia are Shaw's equivalents of Marcus Superbus and Mercia (and their kind). To emphasize this he had the same actress, Lilith McCarthy, who had played Mercia opposite Wilson Barrett, play Lavinia. The meetings between the Captain and Lavinia are strictly parallel to those between Marcus Superbus and Mercia, as in Act I when the Captain fails to persuade Lavinia to 'drop a pinch of incense on the altar' and choose 'a kindly love and an honorable alliance'.

In Act II (as in the final Act of *The Sign of the Cross*) the Roman attempts to persuade the Christian to give up martyrdom. In both plays the attempt is a failure, but Shaw has considerably altered both the tone and the consequences. After Ferrovius has killed the gladiators and Androcles has tamed the lion, Lavinia and the Captain still do not become lovers or agree to marry. Nor does the Captain decide to become a Christian. Instead he continues to serve 'the gods that are' and Lavinia continues to 'strive for the coming of the God who is not yet'.

There are many other similarities between the two plays and an interesting one is the way in which Androcles elects to be thrown to the lions rather than fight the the gladiators. He tells the Editor:

> No, really: I cant fight: I never could: I cant bring myself to dislike anyone enough. I'm to be thrown to the lions with the lady.
>
> (p. 138)

This parallels the case of the young Christian, Stephanus, in *The Sign of the Cross*, who has been tortured and quails at the thought of death. He is left to the lions with the women. Androcles's reasons for not fighting are quite different, as is apparent not only in what he says but what he does.

Setting

The setting of a play is where the action takes place. *Androcles and the Lion* in Acts I and II uses the settings of the first and final Acts of *The Sign of the Cross*. Both commence in the streets of Rome where Christians are being led to the prisons. Both conclude in the area behind the Coliseum where the Christians await their deaths. Here, however, is one of Shaw's significant changes. Whereas *The Sign of the Cross* refers to this setting as a dungeon (emphasizing the theme of persecution) Shaw treats it as a green room (a room in a theatre where actors await their turns on stage, and receive privileged visitors). There is even a Call Boy and an Editor (Stage Manager) to emphasize that the Christians, as far as the Romans are concerned, are part of an entertainment, not victims of a persecution. The gladiators share the same space and the Emperor discusses the finer points of showmanship with them on the way to his box.

One of Shaw's reasons for altering the nature of the setting in this way is to remove the kind of excitement his audiences might have felt when confronted with 'Ancient Rome', usually depicted as full of cruel, lascivious Romans and dungeons full of whips, chains, and tortured Christians. The Puritan imagination has typically allowed representations of sex and violence so long as they are contained within a strong moral tale. Thus it is possible to enjoy and condemn at the same time. Shaw provides the audience with a healthier form of enjoyment.

2 Pantomime and *Androcles and the Lion*

The first performance of Shaw's play was preceded by *The Harlequinade* by D C Calthrop and Granville Barker, described by Shaw as 'a long and hopelessly bad play'. It featured the traditional characters Harlequin, Columbine and Pantaloon, and presented the history of the Harlequinade in dramatic form. Harlequinades were the traditional stuff of pantomime and it was only in the second half of the nineteenth century, when Shaw was still a boy, that pantomime in the format we know today was developed. It is also interesting to note that on occasion the story of Androcles was used as pantomime material.

Scenes

Little imagination is needed to recognize that the clowning between Androcles, Megaera, and the lion in the Prologue and the similar action between Androcles, the lion and the Emperor at the conclusion is related to pantomime. A further similarity is the grand resolution involving the entire cast (with the exception of Spintho and Megaera) in which a happy ending is compulsory, and they all get more or less what they want.

Setting

Pantomime usually opens with a rather bleak scene, and has a conclusion that should be the most magnificent scene and setting of all. Immediately it is obvious that the Prologue which opens *Androcles and the Lion*, involving Androcles, Megaera, and the lion, and set in the dark forest, perfectly fits the traditional pantomime opening. The final transformation scene of pantomime comes at the end of Act II and requires a revolving stage that opens the play out into the Coliseum proper when Androcles goes to face the lion. These two distinctively pantomime settings completely surround the Christian melodrama.

There is, however, a further dimension to this. While it is true that Christian melodrama is usually located in Ancient Rome, the doubtful historical accuracy of its vision of Rome is considerably undermined in this play by the role of Ancient Rome as a pantomime setting. Pantomimes, even when situated in a supposedly real place, such as Dick Whittington's London, always offer fantastic and fanciful versions of the setting. Shaw has exploited this aspect of pantomime setting and underlined it by importing Androcles – who has no part in the Christian story – and a pantomime lion. Shaw's purpose in doing so is twofold. On the one hand it mocks the Christian melodrama version. On the other, by turning Ancient Rome into a fantasy setting and so reducing its historical value, he emphasizes the parallels he can suggest between the world depicted and the Britain of his day. Further to this satirical effect, and because of the timelessness that pantomime lends to his setting, the themes he dramatizes become universalized, and apply to all time. For example, his view of the Roman use of power applies to all governments, now as then, and his rebels are as diverse today as ever, no matter what banner they choose to assemble under. The timelessness injected into the Roman setting emphasizes the continued relevance today of *Androcles and the Lion*. Shaw was experimenting here with the use of various levels of fantasy through which to convey his moral view, a method he was to use more frequently during the remainder of his career.

Structure and theme in Androcles and the Lion

Having identified these two dramatic forms in the play, it is necessary to consider the effect they have upon each other, and recognize that *Androcles and the Lion* is more than the sum of its parts.

Christian melodrama offers an entirely different world-view from pantomime. It is concerned with death, the rejection of this world – this 'vale of tears' – for the joys of the next. Pantomime, through the medium of laughter, returns us to *this* world and demands that we see it in a different, positive light. While pantomime challenge the Christian melodrama view, the latter adds dimensions of meaning to the pantomime. Thus, at the end of the play, when Androcles and the lion walk out with the words 'Whilst we stand together, no cage for you: no slavery for me' (p. 150) there is a sense in which they are walking into Paradise, to a time before (or beyond) Christianity. This is, of course, a fantasy, but it is one that acts as an alternative to the Christian idea of the next world, which, in Shaw's view, is also a fantasy. In this context it is important to consider the values that Androcles represents and acts upon.

Critics have often claimed that the pantomime and the Christian melodrama elements of the play bear little relation, or are at odds with each other. Perhaps you will agree, but before deciding you should consider the combination of Christian melodrama and pantomime as part of the argument of the play, not simply an arbitrary mixture designed to shock and outrage.

Fable and parable

Shaw describes *Androcles and the Lion* as a fable play. It is also a parable. Both these forms of story telling are used to illustrate moral arguments and often use fantastic settings and situations, as in Aesop's *Fables*. The fable element is specifically related to the story of Androcles and its moral may be stated as 'virtue is its own reward'. However, this moral may also be applied to the other characters in a generalized way.

The parable form is directly related to the discussion and dramatization of individual courage and faith – or the lack of them – that dominate the play. All the characters act out different types of courage, and at different levels and through following their own ways achieve various degrees of self knowledge and understanding both of the world and their place in it. Their courage is not only related to their character but also to the nature of their faith. Through the testing of their faith the main characters come to a more real, less romantic, vision of the world. Despite the apparent mockery of religion, *Androcles and the Lion* is a very religious play. Religion and politics are, as we have seen, inseparable for Shaw, and therefore the parable elements extend to the struggle for power between the state and the Christians.

Comedy and the drama of ideas

Critics have tended to look down on comedy as a dramatic form. There are many reasons for this, chiefly the status given to tragedy in our society, and the familiar prejudice that you cannot be laughing, joking, enjoying yourself, and serious at the same time: if you are serious then you will behave seriously! Shaw has a lot of fun with this view of seriousness; his Christians laugh and sing on their way to prison: 'Thats what we have to put up with every day, sir,' the Centurion – a man who clearly believes that religion is a serious business, and therefore nothing to do with laughter – tells the Captain: "Theyre always laughing and joking something scandalous. Theyve no religion: thats how it is" (p. 114). Shaw is laughing here at the conventional view of religion and seriousness. It is part of his long argument against (Victorian) puritanism, contrasting a view of the truly religious sense of pleasure and joy with conventional gloom and contempt for the world, certainly as seen in Christian melodrama. And throughout the play Shaw uses humour to deflate the expectations and ideas of Christianity as it is usually seen.

For like many a comic writer and satirist before him Shaw believed that there is always a truth to be found in a joke – 'many a true word is spoken in jest' – and he commonly deployed varieties of humorous technique in all his plays. In *Androcles and the Lion* we experience a wide range extending from the witty exchange, the comic situation, to the farcical business with Androcles and his lion. Throughout, however, the humour has a point: Shaw was interested in putting across controversial ideas to his audiences in order to make them think. Laughter not only has the entertainment value necessary to convey his ideas through the drama, and to make the audience laugh at their own ideas, but has the value of keeping them attentive, often in spite of themselves.

Characterization

It is often said of Shaw's characters that they are not 'real', that they do not have, in the dramatic sense, a life of their own, meaning partly that they do not surprise us, and partly that they are little more than puppets Shaw has designed to express certain aspects of the argument in his plays. Such criticism has been levelled at the characters of *Androcles and the Lion*. However, the demand for 'real' fully rounded characters is not always reasonable, even in critical terms: for example, farce, comedy, pantomime, and Christian melodrama are forms that rarely, if ever, deploy 'real' characters. Instead they depend upon laughter, wit, comic situations, complicated plots, excitement, extravagant settings, and so on, to engage the audience.

Characters in pantomime, fable, and parable tend to be caricatures, familiar types, even emblematic figures. It is, for example, rather difficult for an actor to be a 'real' person while being chased by a pantomime lion. The simplification of the characters in *Androcles and the Lion* is, in dramatic terms, perfectly legitimate. It is important to see them in the context in which they appear and not to import unreasonable demands from outside. Nevertheless, while it is true that all the characters have their function in the argument Shaw conducts throughout the drama, you may feel that Lavinia, Androcles, Ferrovius, even the Captain, are fleshed out enough for you to engage your sympathies with their desires, ideas and predicaments. Remember, also, that some characters act as comments upon those that appear in various other Christian melodramas, and that others, like Androcles and the Emperor, have to appear in both the pantomime and Christian melodrama parts of the play.

The Captain

The relationship between the Captain and Lavinia represents a central conflict between the Roman (pagan) culture – usually presented as cruel and sensuous – and the persecuted Christians who are shown as humble, charitable, and willing to give up this world for the joys of the next. But it was not Shaw's objective to contrast pagan and Christian in this fashion. Although the Captain and Lavinia have the same conflicts as Marcus Superbus and Mercia (in *The Sign of the Cross*) they never become victims of their emotions in the same way. They treat each other with respect, as equals, and as fellow human beings. Far from being a sensualist himself, the Captain warns Lavinia that

> The men in that audience tomorrow will be the vilest of voluptuaries: men to whom the only passion excited by a beautiful woman is the lust to see her tortured and torn shrieking limb from limb. It is a crime to gratify that passion.
>
> (p. 118)

Later, in Act II, after Lavinia again turns down his offer of marriage, he exclaims:

> What nonsense it all is! And what a monstrous thing that you
> should die for such nonsense ...
>
> (p. 142)

The Captain is first and last a soldier and, he thinks, a realist.
Thus he worships 'the gods that are', but his relationship to
religion is utterly conventional and hollow. His arguments to
Lavinia are directed towards commonsense and respectability.
In many ways they are similar to those Megaera offers Androcles in the Prologue. The Captain is decent but complacent. He
therefore finds himself helpless in this situation. His threat to
cut the Emperor's throat 'and then my own when I see your
blood' may be romantic but it is also futile. Apart from saving
no one, it will change nothing.

Lavinia

No orthodox Christian, nor the typical heroine of a Christian
melodrama, Shaw identifies Lavinia as a 'clever and fearless freethinker' (see p. 152). He means that she is an intelligent woman
determined to reach her own conclusions, and strong enough to
act upon them. As a seeker of knowledge and understanding she
is, for Shaw, a truly religious person. She represents the
Christian as a social rebel. She tells the Captain:

> ... when men who believe neither in my god nor in their
> own – men who do not know the meaning of the word religion
> – when these men drag me to the foot of an iron statue that
> has become the symbol of the terror and darkness through
> which they walk, of their cruelty and greed, of their hatred of
> God and their oppression of man – when they ask me to
> pledge my soul before the people that this hideous idol is God,
> and that all this wickedness and falsehood is divine truth,
> I cannot do it ...
>
> (p. 119)

But there is also a sense of progress in her development as she moves toward a fuller understanding of her own beliefs, and what God means for her. Her willingness to face reality, a reality she equates with 'the God who is not yet', takes Lavinia somewhat outside the bounds of normal Christianity, certainly as represented in *The Sign of the Cross* where the heroine demonstrates an almost masochistic longing for death.

Ferrovius

From his entrance in Act I until he slays the gladiators in Act II, Ferrovius practically dominates the proceedings. This is un-usual for this type of character who normally takes a minor role in a Christian melodrama. (The strong man suited to the life of a soldier, the gentle giant who adopts Christianity is a familiar figure and has his counterpart in *The Sign of the Cross* in the character Melos. There is a similar character in *Quo Vadis?* who, like Ferrovius loses his control under stress.)

In his Afterword Shaw describes Ferrovius as a Pauline Christian, and 'comparatively stupid and conscience ridden'. He also makes considerable play of the fact that an entire nation of Christians – the English – had no trouble in turning itself into soldiers and worshipping Mars (the Roman god of war) rather than Christ. Unlike Ferrovius they do not acknowledge what they are doing: Shaw had a great dislike of vengeance-seeking parsons.

Within his person Ferrovius carries the conflict between the soldier Captain and the Christian Lavinia: they argue with each other, but the same argument rages *within* Ferrovius. When Lavinia tells him that 'Nothing but faith can save you' he answers:

Faith! Which faith? There are two faiths. There is our faith. And there is the warrior's faith, the faith in fighting, the faith

that sees God in the sword. How if that faith should
overwhelm me?

(p. 138)

It has become clear that Ferrovius is struggling throughout
against his real nature in attempting to follow Christ: he can
neither surrender the sword nor burn the incense. The outcome
is inevitable.

Ferrovius's entrance emphasizes the point that although the
Christians (with the exception of Spintho) are all religious in
some way, it is doubtful whether they hold a single common
feature, but exist, rather, as Shaw claims, as a variety of
rebellious people gathered together under the banner of Christianity. This point can also be established by comparing Ferrovius with Androcles. Not only are their characters entirely
different but so is the nature of their religion. Consequently in
Ferrovius, as well as in Lavinia, we witness another major
theme develop, namely, the struggles of each individual through
the spiritual life to find a true understanding of themselves in
the testing of their beliefs against reality.

Spintho

The parallel character in *The Sign of the Cross* is a traitor (Judas
figure) but Shaw presents him as a coward. Martyrdom is an
insurance policy that offers him life after death but he cannot go
through with it. Not only lack of courage but lack of faith
betrays him too. He dies accidentally on his way to the pagan
altar. Spintho not only represents a type of Christianity but acts
as a foil to Ferrovius and Androcles in particular, emphasizing
the nature of their courage and faith.

The Emperor

Naturally the Roman Emperor is an important figure in a
Christian melodrama. In *The Sign of the Cross* it is Nero, regarded

as the worst of them all. Emperors are made to represent the evils of Rome – soft-bellied, lustful and sadistic – in excess. Shaw's Emperor is something of a contrast, being jovial, witty, and sporting – very much a caricature of an English gentleman in fact! Shaw is anxious to make clear a parallel between the Roman Empire and the British Empire in their use of power against those who threaten it. It is also to be understood that the Emperor represents a state of non-religion, and his acceptance of Christianity as the official religion is in no way a triumph for Christianity, as his reasons are entirely irreligious. Like the gladiator who tells him. 'It is all one to us, Caesar', the Emperor is indifferent on the matter of faith.

A further point about the Emperor is that he remains unnamed, thus adding to the sense of non-specific time that Shaw is aiming to achieve.

Androcles

As Shaw notes in his Prefatory Note (p. 103), Androcles has nothing to do with Christian history but is a character taken from a classical tale of Greek origins. To present him as a Christian is a piece of Shavian fantasy. Nonetheless, as a member of the band of Christians, Androcles strongly highlights the variety of religious positions that Shaw has distributed amongst them. He is also the perfect opposite to Ferrovius in character. Androcles appears to represent an almost primitive view of religion that, although it may be compatible at some points with Christianity, could certainly evolve without it.

Though we have already noted a point of similarity between Androcles and the 'innocent child' victim in *The Sign of the Cross* it is more appropriate to note that Androcles is more directly related – like his friend, the lion – to the clowns in the pantomimes of Shaw's youth. One has only to recall such innocent heroes of pantomime as Dick Whittington, to see the similarity. Again, there is a closeness to the clowns of the early cinema, Charlie Chaplin and, more clearly, Buster Keaton.

Shaw skilfully orchestrates his progress through the pantomime opening, weaving his story into that of the Christian
melodrama and back to the pantomime conclusion. The character is sketched lightly, but sufficently for him to achieve
successfully the necessary transitions from one type of situation
to another. He is a simpleton – a word often used to link
innocence and holiness – and he accords with the romantic view
of Saint Francis, even Christ himself. The audience laughs at
him, but although he seems foolish there is a serious edge to his
speech and actions. There is also the suggestion, as he and the
lion walk out of the Coliseum that he represents the meek whom
Christ said would inherit the earth.

The lion

Not surprisingly the lion is often overlooked in a character
analysis but, as one of Shaw's few silent characters, he deserves
the last word here. The lion recognizably belongs to the
pantomime tradition of Puss in Boots and Dick Whittington's
cat (and beyond these to the lion in the play that Bottom and his
friends perform for Duke Theseus in *A Midsummer Night's Dream*
– Shaw's favourite Shakespeare play). However, Androcles's
lion acquires more significance than is normally the case. Apart
from usefully signalling the pantomime sections with his
appearance he becomes something of an emblematic beast
gaining meaning as the play progresses. The point is that
through the many changing facets of the play the lion takes on
many different roles and symbolically stands for many major
themes. For instance it is not difficult to see that the lion stands
for all animals when Androcles pleads with Ferrovius for their
souls. Again, the parable in the play involves an elaborate
presentation through dramatized discussion and action of the
themes of courage and faith involving, in addition, direct
reference to a parallel between Britain and Rome. Lions are

associated with strength and courage – 'lion-hearted'. They are also closely associated with religion – the biblical Lion (and the Lion of Judah). There is also the British Lion. Within these terms the end of the play, when Androcles and the lion walk away unmolested, is more significant and appropriate than might otherwise appear to be the case.

Films

An appalling Hollywood version of Shaw's play was produced in 1952 starring Victor Mature as Androcles and employing trick photography and a real lion.

There is an excellent BBC production (1984) starring Billy Connolly as Androcles and Bernard Breslaw as Ferrovius which is strongly recommended.

The Sign of the Cross was filmed in 1933 starring Charles Laughton as Nero and Claudette Colbert as his queen. Cecil B De Mille directed, and it includes the famous bath in asses' milk scene!

Androcles and the Lion

Characters

in order of their appearance

THE LION
MEGAERA
ANDROCLES
A BATCH OF CHRISTIAN PRISONERS
LAVINIA
THE CENTURION
A CHRISTIAN
THE CAPTAIN
LENTULUS
METELLUS
FERROVIUS
SPINTHO
THE OX DRIVER
THE RETIARIUS
SECUTOR
GLADIATORS
THE CALL BOY
THE EDITOR
THE KEEPER
THE EMPEROR
THREE ATTENDANTS
TWO SLAVES

PREFACE ON THE PROSPECTS OF CHRISTIANITY

Why not give Christianity a Trial?

The question seems a hopeless one after 2000 years of resolute adherence to the old cry of "Not this man, but Barabbas." Yet it is beginning to look as if Barabbas was a failure, in spite of his strong right hand, his victories, his empires, his millions of money, and his moralities and churches and political constitutions. "This man" has not been a failure yet; for nobody has ever been sane enough to try his way. But he has had one quaint triumph. Barabbas has stolen his name and taken his cross as a standard. There is a sort of compliment in that. There is even a sort of loyalty in it, like that of the brigand who breaks every law and yet claims to be a patriotic subject of the king who makes them. We have always had a curious feeling that though we crucified Christ on a stick, he somehow managed to get hold of the right end of it, and that if we were better men we might try his plan. There have been one or two grotesque attempts at it by inadequate people, such as the Kingdom of God in Munster, which was ended by a crucifixion so much more atrocious than the one on Calvary that the bishop who took the part of Annas went home and died of horror. But responsible people have never made such attempts. The moneyed, respectable, capable world has been steadily anti-Christian and Barabbasque since the crucifixion; and the specific doctrine of Jesus has not in all that time been put into political or general social practice. I am no more a Christian than Pilate was, or you, gentle reader; and yet, like Pilate, I greatly prefer Jesus to Annas and Caiaphas; and I am ready to admit that after contemplating the world and human nature for nearly sixty years, I see no way out of the world's misery but the way which would have been found by Christ's will if he had undertaken the work of a modern practical statesman.

Pray do not at this early point lose patience with me and shut the book. I assure you I am as sceptical and scientific and modern a thinker as you will find anywhere. I grant you I know a great deal more about economics and politics than Jesus did, and can do things he could not do. I am by all Barabbasque standards a person of much better character and standing, and greater practical sense. I have no sympathy with vagabonds and talkers who try to reform society by taking men away from their regular productive work and making vagabonds and talkers of them too; and if I had been Pilate I should have recognized as plainly as he the necessity for suppressing attacks on the existing social order, however corrupt that order might be, by people with no knowledge of government and no power to construct political machinery to carry out their views, acting on the very dangerous delusion that the end of the world was at hand. I make no defence of such Christians as Savonarola and John of Leyden: they were scuttling the ship before they had learned how to build a raft; and it became necessary to throw them overboard to save the crew. I say this to set myself right with respectable society; but I must still insist that if Jesus could have worked out the practical problems of a Communist constitution, an admitted obligation to deal with crime without revenge or punishment, and a full assumption by humanity of divine responsibilities, he would have conferred an incalculable benefit on mankind, because these distinctive demands of his are now turning out to be good sense and sound economics.

I say distinctive, because his common humanity and his subjection to time and space (that is, to the Syrian life of his period) involved his belief in many things, true and false, that in no way distinguish him from other Syrians of that time. But such common beliefs do not constitute specific Christianity any more than wearing a beard, working in a carpenter's shop, or believing that the earth is flat and that the stars could drop on it from heaven like hailstones. Christianity interests practical statesmen now because of the doctrines that distinguished Christ from the Jews and the Barabbasques generally, including ourselves.

WHY JESUS MORE THAN ANOTHER?

I do not imply, however, that these doctrines were peculiar to Christ. A doctrine peculiar to one man would be only a craze, unless its comprehension depended on a development of human faculty so rare that only one exceptionally gifted man possessed it. But even in this case it would be useless, because incapable of spreading. Christianity is a step in moral evolution which is independent of any individual preacher. If Jesus had never existed (and that he ever existed in any other sense than that in which Shakespear's Hamlet existed has been vigorously questioned) Tolstoy would have thought and taught and quarrelled with the Greek Church all the same. Their creed has been fragmentarily practised to a considerable extent in spite of the fact that the laws of all countries treat it, in effect, as criminal. Many of its advocates have been militant atheists. But for some reason the imagination of white mankind has picked out Jesus of Nazareth as *the* Christ, and attributed all the Christian doctrines to him; and as it is the doctrine and not the man that matters, and, as, besides, one symbol is as good as another provided everyone attaches the same meaning to it, I raise, for the moment, no question as to how far the gospels are original, and how far they consist of Greek and Chinese interpolations. The record that Jesus said certain things is not invalidated by a demonstration that Confucius said them before him. Those who claim a literal divine paternity for him cannot be silenced by the discovery that the same claim was made for Alexander and Augustus. And I am not just now concerned with the credibility of the gospels as records of fact; for I am not acting as a detective, but turning our modern lights on to certain ideas and doctrines in them which disentangle themselves from the rest because they are flatly contrary to common practice, common sense, and common belief, and yet have, in the teeth of dogged incredulity and recalcitrance, produced an irresistible impression that Christ, though rejected by his posterity as an unpractical dreamer, and executed by his contemporaries as a dangerous anarchist and blasphemous madman, was greater than his judges.

WAS JESUS A COWARD?

I know quite well that this impression of superiority is not produced on everyone, even of those who profess extreme susceptibility to it. Setting aside the huge mass of inculcated Christ-worship which has no real significance because it has no intelligence, there is, among people who are really free to think for themselves on the subject, a great deal of hearty dislike of Jesus and of contempt for his failure to save himself and overcome his enemies by personal bravery and cunning as Mahomet did. I have heard this feeling expressed far more impatiently by persons brought up in England as Christians than by Mahometans, who are, like their prophet, very civil to Jesus, and allow him a place in their esteem and veneration at least as high as we accord to John the Baptist. But this British bulldog contempt is founded on a complete misconception of his reasons for submitting voluntarily to an ordeal of torment and death. The modern Secularist is often so determined to regard Jesus as a man like himself and nothing more, that he slips unconsciously into the error of assuming that Jesus shared that view. But it is quite clear from the New Testament writers (the chief authorities for believing that Jesus ever existed) that Jesus at the time of his death believed himself to be the Christ, a divine personage. It is therefore absurd to criticize his conduct before Pilate as if he were Colonel Roosevelt or Admiral von Tirpitz or even Mahomet. Whether you accept his belief in his divinity as fully as Simon Peter did, or reject it as a delusion which led him to submit to torture and sacrifice his life without resistance in the conviction that he would presently rise again in glory, you are equally bound to admit that, far from behaving like a coward or a sheep, he shewed considerable physical fortitude in going through a cruel ordeal against which he could have defended himself as effectually as he cleared the money-changers out of the temple. "Gentle Jesus, meek and mild" is a snivelling modern invention, with no warrant in the gospels. St Matthew would as soon have thought of applying such adjectives to Judas Maccabeus as to Jesus; and even St Luke, who makes Jesus polite and gracious, does not make him meek. The picture of him as an English curate of the farcical comedy type, too meek to fight a policeman, and everybody's butt, may be useful in the nursery to soften children; but that such a figure could ever have become a centre of the world's attention is too absurd for discussion: grown men and women may speak kindly of a harmless creature who utters amiable sentiments and is a helpless nincompoop when he is called on to defend them; but they will not follow him, nor do what he tells them, because they do not wish to share his defeat and disgrace.

Was Jesus a Martyr?

It is important therefore that we should clear our minds of the notion that Jesus died, as some of us are in the habit of declaring, for his social and political opinions. There have been many martyrs to those opinions; but he was not one of them, nor, as his words shew, did he see any more sense in martyrdom than Galileo did. He was executed by the Jews for the blasphemy of claiming to be a God; and Pilate, to whom this was a mere piece of superstitious nonsense, let them execute him as the cheapest way of keeping them quiet, on the formal plea that he had committed treason against Rome by saying that he was the King of the Jews. He was not falsely accused, nor denied full opportunities of defending himself. The proceedings were quite straightforward and regular; and Pilate, to whom the appeal lay, favored him and despised his judges, and was evidently willing enough to be conciliated. But instead of denying the charge, Jesus repeated the offence. He knew what he was doing: he had alienated numbers of his own disciples and been stoned in the streets for doing it before. He was not lying: he believed literally what he said. The horror of the High Priest was perfectly natural: he was a Primate confronted with a heterodox street preacher uttering what seemed to him an appalling and impudent blasphemy. The fact that the blasphemy was to Jesus a simple statement of fact, and that it has since been accepted as such by all western nations, does not invalidate the proceedings, nor give us the right to regard Annas and Caiaphas as worse men than the Archbishop of Canterbury and the Head Master of Eton. If Jesus had been indicted in a modern court, he would have been examined by two doctors; found to be obsessed by a delusion; declared incapable of pleading; and sent to an asylum: that is the whole difference. But please note that when a man is charged before a modern tribunal (to take a case that happened the other day) of having asserted and maintained that he was an officer returned from the front to receive the Victoria Cross at the hands of the King, although he was in fact a mechanic, nobody thinks of treating him as afflicted with a delusion. He is punished for false pretences, because his assertion is credible and therefore misleading. Just so, the claim to divinity made by Jesus was to the High Priest, who looked forward to the coming of a Messiah, one that might conceivably have been true, and might therefore have misled the people in a very dangerous way. That was why he treated Jesus as an impostor and a blasphemer where we should have treated him as a madman.

THE GOSPELS WITHOUT PREJUDICE

All this will become clear if we read the gospels without prejudice. When I was young it was impossible to read them without fantastic confusion of thought. The confusion was so utterly confounded that it was called the proper spirit to read the Bible in. Jesus was a baby; and he was older than creation. He was a man who could be persecuted, stoned, scourged, and killed; and he was a god, immortal and all-powerful, able to raise the dead and call millions of angels to his aid. It was a sin to doubt either view of him: that is, it was a sin to reason about him; and the end was that you did not reason about him, and read about him only when you were compelled. When you heard the gospel stories read in church, or learnt them from painters and poets, you came out with an impression of their contents that would have astonished a Chinaman who had read the story without prepossession. Even sceptics who were specially on their guard, put the Bible in the dock, and read the gospels with the object of detecting discrepancies in the four narratives to shew that the writers were as subject to error as the writers of yesterday's newspaper.

All this has changed greatly within two generations. Today the Bible is so little read that the language of the Authorized Version is rapidly becoming obsolete; so that even in the United States, where the old tradition of the verbal infallibility of "the book of books" lingers more strongly than anywhere else except perhaps in Ulster, retranslations into modern English have been introduced perforce to save its bare intelligibility. It is quite easy today to find cultivated persons who have never read the New Testament, and on whom therefore it is possible to try the experiment of asking them to read the gospels and state what they have gathered as to the history and views and character of Christ.

The Gospels now Unintelligible to Novices

But it will not do to read the gospels with a mind furnished only for the reception of, say, a biography of Goethe. You will not make sense of them, nor even be able without impatient weariness to persevere in the task of going steadily through them, unless you know something of the history of the human imagination as applied to religion. Not long ago I asked a writer of distinguished intellectual competence whether he had made a study of the gospels since his childhood. His reply was that he had lately tried, but "found it all such nonsense that I could not stick it." As I do not want to send anyone to the gospels with this result, I had better here give a brief exposition of how much of the history of religion is needed to make the gospels and the conduct and ultimate fate of Jesus intelligible and interesting.

WORLDLINESS OF THE MAJORITY

The first common mistake to get rid of is that mankind consists of a great mass of religious people and a few eccentric atheists. It consists of a huge mass of worldly people, and a small percentage of persons deeply interested in religion and concerned about their own souls and other people's; and this section consists mostly of those who are passionately affirming the established religion and those who are passionately attacking it, the genuine philosophers being very few. Thus you never have a nation of millions of Wesleys and one Tom Paine. You have a million Mr Worldly Wisemans, one Wesley, with his small congregation, and one Tom Paine, with *his* smaller congregation. The passionately religious are a people apart; and if they were not hopelessly outnumbered by the worldly, they would turn the world upside down, as St Paul was reproached, quite justly, for wanting to do. Few people can number among their personal acquaintances a single atheist or a single Plymouth Brother. Unless a religious turn in ourselves has led us to seek the little Societies to which these rare birds belong, we pass our lives among people who, whatever creeds they may repeat, and in whatever temples they may avouch their respectability and wear their Sunday clothes, have robust consciences, and hunger and thirst, not for righteousness, but for rich feeding and comfort and social position and attractive mates and ease and pleasure and respect and consideration: in short, for love and money. To these people one morality is as good as another provided they are used to it and can put up with its restrictions without unhappiness; and in the maintenance of this morality they will fight and punish and coerce without scruple. They may not be the salt of the earth, these Philistines; but they are the substance of civilization; and they save society from ruin by criminals and conquerors as well as by Savonarolas and Knipperdollings. And as they know, very sensibly, that a little religion is good for children and serves morality, keeping the poor in goodhumor or in awe by promising rewards in heaven or threatening torments in hell, they encourage the religious people up to a certain point: for instance, if Savonarola only tells the ladies of Florence that they ought to tear off their jewels and finery and sacrifice them to God, they offer him a cardinal's hat, and praise him as a saint; but if he induces them to actually do it, they burn him as a public nuisance.

RELIGION OF THE MINORITY. SALVATIONISM

The religion of the tolerated religious minority has always been essentially the same religion: that is why its changes of name and form have made so little difference. That is why, also, a nation so civilized as the English can convert negroes to their faith with great ease, but cannot convert Mahometans or Jews. The negro finds in civilized Salvationism an unspeakably more comforting version of his crude creed; but neither Saracen nor Jew sees any advantage in it over his own version. The Crusader was surprised to find the Saracen quite as religious and moral as himself, and rather more than less civilized. The Latin Christian has nothing to offer the Greek Christian that Greek Christianity has not already provided. They are all, at root, Salvationists.

Let us trace this religion of Salvation from its beginnings. So many things that man does not himself contrive or desire are always happening: death, plagues, tempests, blights, floods, sunrise and sunset, growths and harvests and decay, and Kant's two wonders of the starry heavens above us and the moral law within us, that we conclude that somebody must be doing it all, or that somebody is doing the good and somebody else doing the evil, or that armies of invisible persons, beneficent and malevolent, are doing it; hence you postulate gods and devils, angels and demons. You propitiate these powers with presents, called sacrifices, and flatteries, called praises. Then the Kantian moral law within you makes you conceive your god as a judge; and straightway you try to corrupt him, also with presents and flatteries. This seems shocking to us; but our objection to it is quite a recent development: no longer ago than Shakespear's time it was thought quite natural that litigants should give presents to human judges; and the buying off of divine wrath by actual money payments to priests, or, in the reformed churches which discountenance this, by subscriptions to charities and church building and the like, is still in full swing. Its practical disadvantage is that though it makes matters very easy for the rich, it cuts off the poor from all hope of divine favor. And this quickens the moral criticism of the poor to such an extent, that they soon find the moral law within them revolting against the idea of buying off the deity with gold and gifts, though are still quite ready to buy him off with the paper money of praise and professions of repentance. Accordingly, you will find that though a religion may last unchanged for many centuries in primitive communities where the conditions of life leave no room for poverty and riches, and the process of propitiating the supernatural powers is as well within the means of the least of the members as within those of the headman, yet when commercial civilization arrives, and capitalism divides the people into a few rich and a great many so poor that they can barely live, a movement for religious reform will arise among the poor, and will be essentially a movement for cheap or entirely gratuitous salvation.

To understand what the poor mean by propitiation, we must examine for a moment what they mean by justice.

THE DIFFERENCE BETWEEN ATONEMENT AND PUNISHMENT

The primitive idea of justice is partly legalized revenge and partly expiation by sacrifice. It works out from both sides in the notion that two blacks make a white, and that when a wrong has been done, it should be paid for by an equivalent suffering. It seems to the Philistine majority a matter of course that this compensating suffering should be inflicted on the wrongdoer for the sake of its deterrent effect on other would-be wrongdoers; but a moment's reflection will shew that this utilitarian application corrupts the whole transaction. For example, the shedding of innocent blood cannot be balanced by the shedding of guilty blood. Sacrificing a criminal to propitiate God for the murder of one of his righteous servants is like sacrificing a mangy sheep or an ox with the rinderpest: it calls down divine wrath instead of appeasing it. In doing it we offer God as a sacrifice the gratification of our own revenge and the protection of our own lives without cost to ourselves; and cost to ourselves is the essence of sacrifice and expiation. However much the Philistines have succeeded in confusing these things in practice, they are to the Salvationist sense distinct and even contrary. The Baronet's cousin in Dickens's novel, who, perplexed by the failure of the police to discover the murderer of the baronet's solicitor, said "Far better hang wrong fellow than no fellow," was not only expressing a very common sentiment, but trembling on the brink of the rarer Salvationist opinion that it is much better to hang the wrong fellow: that, in fact, the wrong fellow is the right fellow to hang.

The point is a cardinal one, because until we grasp it not only does historical Christianity remain unintelligible to us, but those who do not care a rap about historical Christianity may be led into the mistake of supposing that if we discard revenge, and treat murderers exactly as God treated Cain: that is, exempt them from punishment by putting a brand on them as unworthy to be sacrificed, and let them face the world as best they can with that brand on them, we should get rid both of punishment and sacrifice. It would not at all follow: on the contrary, the feeling that there must be an expiation of the murder might quite possibly lead to our putting some innocent person—the more innocent the better—to a cruel death to balance the account with divine justice.

B

ANDROCLES AND THE LION

Salvation at first a Class Privilege; and the Remedy

Thus, even when the poor decide that the method of purchasing salvation by offering rams and goats or bringing gold to the altar must be wrong because they cannot afford it, we still do not feel "saved" without a sacrifice and a victim. In vain do we try to substitute mystical rites that cost nothing, such as circumcision, or, as a substitute for that, baptism. Our sense of justice still demands an expiation, a sacrifice, a sufferer for our sins. And this leaves the poor man still in his old difficulty; for if it was impossible for him to procure rams and goats and shekels, how much more impossible is it for him to find a neighbor who will voluntarily suffer for his sins: one who will say cheerfully "You have committed a murder. Well, never mind: I am willing to be hanged for it in your stead"?

Our imagination must come to our rescue. Why not, instead of driving ourselves to despair by insisting on a separate atonement by a separate redeemer for every sin, have one great atonement and one great redeemer to compound for the sins of the world once for all? Nothing easier, nothing cheaper. The yoke is easy, the burden light. All you have to do when the redeemer is once found (or invented by the imagination) is to believe in the efficacy of the transaction, and you are saved. The rams and goats cease to bleed; the altars which ask for expensive gifts and continually renewed sacrifices are torn down; and the Church of the single redeemer and the single atonement rises on the ruins of the old temples, and becomes a single Church of the Christ.

Retrospective Atonement; and the Expectation of the Redeemer

But this does not happen at once. Between the old costly religion of the rich and the new gratuitous religion of the poor there comes an interregnum in which the redeemer, though conceived by the human imagination, is not yet found. He is awaited and expected under the names of the Christ, the Messiah, Baldur the Beautiful, or what not; but he has not yet come. Yet the sinners are not therefore in despair. It is true that they cannot say, as we say, "The Christ has come, and has redeemed us"; but they can say "The Christ will come, and will redeem us," which, as the atonement is conceived as retrospective, is equally consoling. There are periods when nations are seething with this expectation and crying aloud with prophecy of the Redeemer through their poets. To feel that atmosphere we have only to take up the Bible and read Isaiah at one end of such a period and Luke and John at the other.

COMPLETION OF THE SCHEME BY LUTHER AND CALVIN

We now see our religion as a quaint but quite intelligible evolution from crude attempts to propitiate the destructive forces of Nature among savages to a subtle theology with a costly ritual of sacrifice possible only to the rich as a luxury, and finally to the religion of Luther and Calvin. And it must be said for the earlier forms that they involved very real sacrifices. The sacrifice was not always vicarious, and is not yet universally so. In India men pay with their own skins, torturing themselves hideously to attain holiness. In the west, saints amazed the world with their austerities and self-scourgings and confessions and vigils. But Luther delivered us from all that. His reformation was a triumph of imagination and a triumph of cheapness. It brought you complete salvation and asked you for nothing but faith. Luther did not know what he was doing in the scientific sociological way in which we know it; but his instinct served him better than knowledge could have done; for it was instinct rather than theological casuistry that made him hold so resolutely to Justification by Faith as the trump card by which he should beat the Pope, or, as he would have put it, the sign in which he should conquer. He may be said to have abolished the charge for admission to heaven. Paul had advocated this; but Luther and Calvin did it.

ANDROCLES AND THE LION

John Barleycorn

There is yet another page in the history of religion which must be conned and digested before the career of Jesus can be fully understood. People who can read long books will find it in Frazer's Golden Bough. Simpler folk will find it in the peasant's song of John Barleycorn, now made accessible to our drawing room amateurs in the admirable collections of Somersetshire Folk Songs by Mr Cecil Sharp. From Frazer's *magnum opus* you will learn how the same primitive logic which makes the Englishman believe today that by eating a beefsteak he can acquire the strength and courage of the bull, and to hold that belief in the face of the most ignominious defeats by vegetarian wrestlers and racers and bicyclists, led the first men who conceived God as capable of incarnation to believe that they could acquire a spark of his divinity by eating his flesh and drinking his blood. And from the song of John Barleycorn you may learn how the miracle of the seed, the growth, and the harvest, still the most wonderful of all the miracles and as inexplicable as ever, taught the primitive husbandman, and, as we must now affirm, taught him quite rightly, that God is in the seed, and that God is immortal. And thus it became the test of Godhead that nothing that you could do to it could kill it, and that when you buried it, it would rise again in renewed life and beauty and give mankind eternal life on condition that it was eaten and drunk, and again slain and buried, to rise again for ever and ever. You may, and indeed must, use John Barleycorn "right barbarouslee," cutting him "off at knee" with your scythes, scourging him with your flails, burying him in the earth; and he will not resist you nor reproach you, but will rise again in golden beauty amidst a great burst of sunshine and bird music, and save you and renew your life. And from the interweaving of these two traditions with the craving for the Redeemer, you at last get the conviction that when the Redeemer comes he will be immortal; he will give us his body to eat and his blood to drink; and he will prove his divinity by suffering a barbarous death without resistance or reproach, and rise from the dead and return to the earth in glory as the giver of life eternal.

LOOKING FOR THE END OF THE WORLD

Yet another persistent belief has beset the imagination of the religious ever since religion spread among the poor, or, rather, ever since commercial civilization produced a hopelessly poor class cut off from enjoyment in this world. That belief is that the end of this world is at hand, and that it will presently pass away and be replaced by a kingdom of happiness, justice, and bliss in which the rich and the oppressors and the unjust shall have no share. We are all familiar with this expectation: many of us cherish some pious relative who sees in every great calamity a sign of the approaching end. Warning pamphlets are in constant circulation: advertisements are put in the papers and paid for by those who are convinced, and who are horrified at the indifference of the irreligious to the approaching doom. And revivalist preachers, now as in the days of John the Baptist, seldom fail to warn their flocks to watch and pray, as the great day will steal upon them like a thief in the night, and cannot be long deferred in a world so wicked. This belief also associates itself with Barleycorn's second coming; so that the two events become identified at last.

There is the other and more artificial side of this belief, on which it is an inculcated dread. The ruler who appeals to the prospect of heaven to console the poor and keep them from insurrection also curbs the vicious by threatening them with hell. In the Koran we find Mahomet driven more and more to this expedient of government; and experience confirms his evident belief that it is impossible to govern without it in certain phases of civilization. We shall see later on that it gives a powerful attraction to the belief in a Redeemer, since it adds to remorse of conscience, which hardened men bear very lightly, a definite dread of hideous and eternal torture.

ANDROCLES AND THE LION

The Honor of Divine Parentage

One more tradition must be noted. The consummation of praise for a king is to declare that he is the son of no earthly father, but of a god. His mother goes into the temple of Apollo, and Apollo comes to her in the shape of a serpent, or the like. The Roman emperors, following the example of Augustus, claimed the title of God. Illogically, such divine kings insist a good deal on their royal human ancestors. Alexander, claiming to be the son of Apollo, is equally determined to be the son of Philip. As the gospels stand, St Matthew and St Luke give genealogies (the two are different) establishing the descent of Jesus through Joseph from the royal house of David, and yet declare that not Joseph but the Holy Ghost was the father of Jesus. It is therefore now held that the story of the Holy Ghost is a later interpolation borrowed from the Greek and Roman imperial tradition. But experience shews that simultaneous faith in the descent from David and the conception by the Holy Ghost is possible. Such double beliefs are entertained by the human mind without uneasiness or consciousness of the contradiction involved. Many instances might be given: a familiar one to my generation being that of the Tichborne claimant, whose attempt to pass himself off as a baronet was supported by an association of laborers on the ground that the Tichborne family, in resisting it, were trying to do a laborer out of his rights. It is quite possible that Matthew and Luke may have been unconscious of the contradiction: indeed the interpolation theory does not remove the difficulty, as the interpolators themselves must have been unconscious of it. A better ground for suspecting interpolation is that St Paul knew nothing of the divine birth, and taught that Jesus came into the world at his birth as the son of Joseph, but rose from the dead after three days as the son of God. Here again, few notice the discrepancy: the three views are accepted simultaneously without intellectual discomfort. We can provisionally entertain half a dozen contradictory versions of an event if we feel either that it does not greatly matter, or that there is a category attainable in which the contradictions are reconciled.

But that is not the present point. All that need be noted here is that the legend of divine birth was sure to be attached sooner or later to very eminent persons in Roman imperial times, and that modern theologians, far from discrediting it, have very logically affirmed the miraculous conception not only of Jesus but of his mother.

With no more scholarly equipment than a knowledge of these habits of the human imagination, anyone may now read the four gospels without bewilderment, and without the contemptuous incredulity which spoils the temper of many modern atheists, or the senseless credulity which sometimes makes pious people force us to shove them aside in emergencies as impracticable lunatics when they ask us to meet violence and injustice with dumb submission in the belief that the strange demeanor of Jesus before Pilate was meant as an example of normal human conduct. Let us admit that without the proper clues the gospels are, to a modern educated person, nonsensical and incredible, whilst the apostles are unreadable. But with the clues, they are fairly plain sailing. Jesus becomes an intelligible and consistent person. His reasons for going "like a lamb to the slaughter" instead of saving himself as Mahomet did, become quite clear. The narrative becomes as credible as any other historical narrative of its period.

MATTHEW

THE ANNUNCIATION: THE MASSACRE: THE FLIGHT

Let us begin with the gospel of Matthew, bearing in mind that it does not profess to be the evidence of an eyewitness. It is a chronicle, founded, like other chronicles, on such evidence and records as the chronicler could get hold of. The only one of the evangelists who professes to give first-hand evidence as an eyewitness naturally takes care to say so; and the fact that Matthew makes no such pretension, and writes throughout as a chronicler, makes it clear that he is telling the story of Jesus as Holinshed told the story of Macbeth, except that, for a reason to be given later on, he must have collected his material and completed his book within the lifetime of persons contemporary with Jesus. Allowance must also be made for the fact that the gospel is written in the Greek language, whilst the first-hand traditions and the actual utterances of Jesus must have been in Aramaic, the dialect of Palestine. These distinctions are important, as you will find if you read Holinshed or Froissart and then read Benvenuto Cellini. You do not blame Holinshed or Froissart for believing and repeating the things they had read or been told, though you cannot always believe these things yourself. But when Cellini tells you that he saw this or did that, and you find it impossible to believe him, you lose patience with him, and are disposed to doubt everything in his autobiography. Do not forget, then, that Matthew is Holinshed and not Benvenuto. The very first pages of his narrative will put your attitude to the test.

Matthew tells us that the mother of Jesus was betrothed to a man of royal pedigree named Joseph, who was rich enough to live in a house in Bethlehem to which kings could bring gifts of gold without provoking any comment. An angel announces to Joseph that Jesus is the son of the Holy Ghost, and that he must not accuse her of infidelity because of her bearing a son of which he is not the father; but this episode disappears from the subsequent narrative: there is no record of its having been told to Jesus, nor any indication of his having any knowledge of it. The narrative, in fact, proceeds in all respects as if the annunciation formed no part of it.

Herod the Tetrarch, believing that a child has been born who will destroy him, orders all the male children to be slaughtered; and Jesus escapes by the flight of his parents into Egypt, whence they return to Nazareth when the danger is over. Here it is necessary to anticipate a little by saying that none of the other evangelists accepts this story, as none of them except John, who throws over Matthew altogether, shares his craze for treating history and biography as mere records of the fulfilment of ancient Jewish prophecies. This craze no doubt led him to seek for some legend bearing out Hosea's "Out of Egypt have I called my son," and Jeremiah's Rachel weeping for her children: in fact, he says so. Nothing that interests us nowadays turns on the credibility of the massacre of the innocents and the flight into Egypt. We may forget them, and proceed to the important part of the narrative, which skips at once to the manhood of Jesus.

John the Baptist

At this moment, a Salvationist prophet named John is stirring the people very strongly. John has declared that the rite of circumcision is insufficient as a dedication of the individual to God, and has substituted the rite of baptism. To us, who are accustomed to baptism as a matter of course, and to whom circumcision is a rather ridiculous foreign practice of no consequence, the sensational effect of such a heresy as this on the Jews is not apparent: it seems to us as natural that John should have baptized people as that the rector of our village should do so. But, as St Paul found to his cost later on, the discarding of circumcision for baptism was to the Jews as startling a heresy as the discarding of transubstantiation in the Mass was to the Catholics of the XVI century.

Jesus joins the Baptists

Jesus entered as a man of thirty (Luke says) into the religious life of his time by going to John the Baptist and demanding baptism from him, much as certain well-to-do young gentlemen forty years ago "joined the Socialists." As far as established Jewry was concerned, he burnt his boats by this action, and cut himself off from the routine of wealth, respectability, and orthodoxy. He then began preaching John's gospel, which, apart from the heresy of baptism, the value of which lay in its bringing the Gentiles (that is, the uncircumcized) within the pale of salvation, was a call to the people to repent of their sins, as the kingdom of heaven was at hand. Luke adds that he also preached the communism of charity; told the surveyors of taxes not to over-assess the taxpayers; and advised soldiers to be content with their wages and not to be violent or lay false accusations. There is no record of John going beyond this.

THE SAVAGE JOHN AND THE CIVILIZED JESUS

Jesus went beyond it very rapidly, according to Matthew. Though, like John, he became an itinerant preacher, he departed widely from John's manner of life. John went into the wilderness, not into the synagogues; and his baptismal font was the river Jordan. He was an ascetic, clothed in skins and living on locusts and wild honey, practising a savage austerity. He courted martyrdom, and met it at the hands of Herod. Jesus saw no merit either in asceticism or martyrdom. In contrast to John he was essentially a highly-civilized, cultivated person. According to Luke, he pointed out the contrast himself, chaffing the Jews for complaining that John must be possessed by the devil because he was a teetotaller and vegetarian, whilst, because Jesus was neither one nor the other, they reviled him as a gluttonous man and a winebibber, the friend of the officials and their mistresses. He told straitlaced disciples that they would have trouble enough from other people without making any for themselves, and that they should avoid martyrdom and enjoy themselves whilst they had the chance. "When they persecute you in this city," he says, "flee into the next." He preaches in the synagogues and in the open air indifferently, just as they come. He repeatedly says, "I desire mercy and not sacrifice," meaning evidently to clear himself of the inveterate superstition that suffering is gratifying to God. "Be not, as the Pharisees, of a sad countenance," he says. He is convivial, feasting with Roman officials and sinners. He is careless of his person, and is remonstrated with for not washing his hands before sitting down to table. The followers of John the Baptist, who fast, and who expect to find the Christians greater ascetics than themselves, are disappointed at finding that Jesus and his twelve friends do not fast; and Jesus tells them that they should rejoice in him instead of being melancholy. He is jocular, and tells them they will all have as much fasting as they want soon enough, whether they like it or not. He is not afraid of disease, and dines with a leper. A woman, apparently to protect him against infection, pours a costly unguent on his head, and is rebuked because what it cost might have been given to the poor. He poohpoohs that lowspirited view, and says, as he said when he was reproached for not fasting, that the poor are always there to be helped, but that he is not there to be anointed always, implying that you should never lose a chance of being happy when there is so much misery in the world. He breaks the Sabbath; is impatient of conventionality when it is uncomfortable or obstructive; and outrages the feelings of the Jews by breaches of it. He is apt to accuse people who feel that way of hypocrisy. Like the late Samuel Butler, he regards disease as a department of sin, and on curing a lame man, says "Thy sins are forgiven" instead of "Arise and walk," subsequently maintaining, when the Scribes reproach him for assuming power to forgive sin as well as to cure disease, that the two come to the same thing. He has no modest affectations, and claims to be greater than Solomon or Jonah. When reproached, as Bunyan was, for resorting to the art of fiction when teaching in parables, he justifies himself on the ground that art is the only way in which the people can be taught. He is, in short, what we should call an artist and a Bohemian in his manner of life.

JESUS NOT A PROSELYTIST

A point of considerable practical importance today is that he expressly repudiates the idea that forms of religion, once rooted, can be weeded out and replanted with the flowers of a foreign faith. "If you try to root up the tares you will root up the wheat as well." Our proselytizing missionary enterprises are thus flatly contrary to his advice; and their results appear to bear him out in his view that if you convert a man brought up in another creed, you inevitably demoralize him. He acts on this view himself, and does not convert his disciples from Judaism to Christianity. To this day a Christian would be in religion a Jew initiated by baptism instead of circumcision, and accepting Jesus as the Messiah, and his teachings as of higher authority than those of Moses, but for the action of the Jewish priests, who, to save Jewry from being submerged in the rising flood of Christianity after the capture of Jerusalem and the destruction of the Temple, set up what was practically a new religious order, with new Scriptures and elaborate new observances, and to their list of the accursed added one Jeschu, a bastard magician, whose comic rogueries brought him to a bad end like Punch or Til Eulenspiegel: an invention which cost them dear when the Christians got the upper hand of them politically. The Jew as Jesus, himself a Jew, knew him, never dreamt of such things, and could follow Jesus without ceasing to be a Jew.

THE TEACHINGS OF JESUS

So much for his personal life and temperament. His public career as a popular preacher carries him equally far beyond John the Baptist. He lays no stress on baptism or vows, and preaches conduct incessantly. He advocates communism, the widening of the private family with its cramping ties into the great family of mankind under the fatherhood of God, the abandonment of revenge and punishment, the countcracting of evil by good instead of by a hostile evil, and an organic conception of society in which you are not an independent individual but a member of society, your neighbor being another member, and each of you members one of another, as two fingers on a hand, the obvious conclusion being that unless you love your neighbor as yourself and he reciprocates you will both be the worse for it. He conveys all this with extraordinary charm, and entertains his hearers with fables (parables) to illustrate them. He has no synagogue or regular congregation, but travels from place to place with twelve men whom he has called from their work as he passed, and who have abandoned it to follow him.

THE MIRACLES

He has certain abnormal powers by which he can perform miracles. He is ashamed of these powers, but, being extremely compassionate, cannot refuse to exercise them when afflicted people beg him to cure them, when multitudes of people are hungry, and when his disciples are terrified by storms on the lakes. He asks for no reward, but begs the people not to mention these powers of his. There are two obvious reasons for his dislike of being known as a worker of miracles. One is the natural objection of all men who possess such powers, but have far more important business in the world than to exhibit them, to be regarded primarily as charlatans, besides being pestered to give exhibitions to satisfy curiosity. The other is that his view of the effect of miracles upon his mission is exactly that taken later on by Rousseau. He perceives that they will discredit him and divert attention from his doctrine by raising an entirely irrelevant issue between his disciples and his opponents.

Possibly my readers may not have studied Rousseau's Letters Written From The Mountain, which may be regarded as the classic work on miracles as credentials of divine mission. Rousseau shews, as Jesus foresaw, that the miracles are the main obstacle to the acceptance of Christianity, because their incredibility (if they were not incredible they would not be miracles) makes people sceptical as to the whole narrative, credible enough in the main, in which they occur, and suspicious of the doctrine with which they are thus associated. "Get rid of the miracles," said Rousseau, "and the whole world will fall at the feet of Jesus Christ." He points out that miracles offered as evidence of divinity, and failing to convince, make divinity ridiculous. He says, in effect, there is nothing in making a lame man walk: thousands of lame men have been cured and have walked without any miracle. Bring me a man with only one leg and make another grow instantaneously on him before my eyes, and I will be really impressed; but mere cures of ailments that have often been cured before are quite useless as evidence of anything else than desire to help and power to cure.

Jesus, according to Matthew, agreed so entirely with Rousseau, and felt the danger so strongly, that when people who were not ill or in trouble came to him and asked him to exercise his powers as a sign of his mission, he was irritated beyond measure, and refused with an indignation which they, not seeing Rousseau's point, must have thought very unreasonable. To be called "an evil and adulterous generation" merely for asking a miracle worker to give an exhibition of his powers, is rather a startling experience. Mahomet, by the way, also lost his temper when people asked him to perform miracles. But Mahomet expressly disclaimed any unusual powers; whereas it is clear from Matthew's story that Jesus (unfortunately for himself, as he thought) had some powers of healing. It is also obvious that the exercise of such powers would give rise to wild tales of magical feats which would expose their hero to condemnation as an impostor among people whose good opinion was of great consequence to the movement started by his mission.

But the deepest annoyance arising from the miracles would be the irrelevance of the issue raised by them. Jesus's teaching has nothing to do with miracles. If his mission had been simply to demonstrate a new method of restoring lost eyesight, the miracle of curing the blind would have been entirely relevant. But to say "You should love your enemies; and to convince you of this I will now proceed to cure this gentleman of cataract" would have been, to a man of Jesus's intelligence, the proposition of an idiot. If it could be proved today that not one of the miracles of Jesus actually occurred, that proof would not invalidate a single one of his didactic utterances; and conversely, if it could be proved that not only did the miracles actually occur, but that he had wrought a thousand other miracles a thousand times more wonderful, not a jot of weight would be added to his doctrine. And yet the intellectual energy of sceptics and divines has been wasted for generations in arguing about the miracles on the assumption that Christianity is at stake in the controversy as to whether the stories of Matthew are false or true. According to Matthew himself, Jesus must have known this only too well; for wherever he went he was assailed with a clamor for miracles, though his doctrine created bewilderment.

So much for the miracles! Matthew tells us further, that Jesus declared that his doctrines would be attacked by Church and State, and that the common multitude were the salt of the earth and the light of the world. His disciples, in their relations with the political and ecclesiastical organizations, would be as sheep among wolves.

MATTHEW IMPUTES BIGOTRY TO JESUS

Matthew, like most biographers, strives to identify the opinions and prejudices of his hero with his own. Although he describes Jesus as tolerant even to carelessness, he draws the line at the Gentile, and represents Jesus as a bigoted Jew who regards his mission as addressed exclusively to "the lost sheep of the house of Israel." When a woman of Canaan begged Jesus to cure her daughter, he first refused to speak to her, and then told her brutally that "It is not meet to take the children's bread and cast it to the dogs." But when the woman said, "Truth, Lord; yet the dogs eat of the crumbs which fall from their master's table," she melted the Jew out of him and made Christ a Christian. To the woman whom he had just called a dog he said, "O woman, great is thy faith: be it unto thee even as thou wilt." This is somehow one of the most touching stories in the gospel; perhaps because the woman rebukes the prophet by a touch of his own finest quality. It is certainly out of character; but as the sins of good men are always out of character, it is not safe to reject the story as invented in the interest of Matthew's determination that Jesus shall have nothing to do with the Gentiles. At all events, there the story is; and it is by no means the only instance in which Matthew reports Jesus, in spite of the charm of his preaching, as extremely uncivil in private intercourse.

THE GREAT CHANGE

So far the history is that of a man sane and interesting apart from his special gifts as orator, healer, and prophet. But a startling change occurs. One day, after the disciples have discouraged him for a long time by their misunderstandings of his mission, and their speculations as to whether he is one of the old prophets come again, and if so, which, his disciple Peter suddenly solves the problem by exclaiming, "Thou art the Christ, the son of the living God." At this Jesus is extraordinarily pleased and excited. He declares that Peter has had a revelation straight from God. He makes a pun on Peter's name, and declares him the founder of his Church. And he accepts his destiny as a god by announcing that he will be killed when he goes to Jerusalem; for if he is really the Christ, it is a necessary part of his legendary destiny that he shall be slain. Peter, not understanding this, rebukes him for what seems mere craven melancholy; and Jesus turns fiercely on him and cries, "Get thee behind me, Satan."

Jesus now becomes obsessed with a conviction of his divinity, and talks about it continually to his disciples, though he forbids them to mention it to others. They begin to dispute among themselves as to the position they shall occupy in heaven when his kingdom is established. He rebukes them strenuously for this, and repeats his teaching that greatness means service and not domination; but he himself, always instinctively somewhat haughty, now becomes arrogant, dictatorial, and even abusive, never replying to his critics without an insulting epithet, and even cursing a fig-tree which disappoints him when he goes to it for fruit. He assumes all the traditions of the folk-lore gods, and announces that, like John Barleycorn, he will be barbarously slain and buried, but will rise from the earth and return to life. He attaches to himself the immemorial tribal ceremony of eating the god, by blessing bread and wine and handing them to his disciples with the words "This is my body: this is my blood." He forgets his own teaching and threatens eternal fire and eternal punishment. He announces, in addition to his Barleycorn resurrection, that he will come to the world a second time in glory and establish his kingdom on earth. He fears that this may lead to the appearance of impostors claiming to be himself, and declares explicitly and repeatedly that no matter what wonders these impostors may perform, his own coming will be unmistakeable, as the stars will fall from heaven, and trumpets be blown by angels. Further he declares that this will take place during the lifetime of persons then present.

JERUSALEM AND THE MYSTICAL SACRIFICE

In this new frame of mind he at last enters Jerusalem amid great popular curiosity; drives the moneychangers and sacrifice sellers out of the temple in a riot; refuses to interest himself in the beauties and wonders of the temple building on the ground that presently not a stone of it shall be left on another; reviles the high priests and elders in intolerable terms; and is arrested by night in a garden to avoid a popular disturbance. He makes no resistance, being persuaded that it is part of his destiny as a god to be murdered and to rise again. One of his followers shews fight, and cuts off the ear of one of his captors. Jesus rebukes him, but does not attempt to heal the wound, though he declares that if he wished to resist he could easily summon twelve million angels to his aid. He is taken before the high priest and by him handed over to the Roman governor, who is puzzled by his silent refusal to defend himself in any way, or to contradict his accusers or their wit-

c

27

nesses, Pilate having naturally no idea that the prisoner conceives himself as going through an inevitable process of torment, death, and burial as a prelude to resurrection. Before the high priest he has also been silent except that when the priest asks him is he the Christ, the Son of God, he replies that they shall all see the Son of Man sitting at the right hand of power, and coming on the clouds of heaven. He maintains this attitude with frightful fortitude whilst they scourge him, mock him, torment him, and finally crucify him between two thieves. His prolonged agony of thirst and pain on the cross at last breaks his spirit, and he dies with a cry of "My God: why hast Thou forsaken me?"

NOT THIS MAN BUT BARABBAS

Meanwhile he has been definitely rejected by the people as well as by the priests. Pilate, pitying him, and unable to make out exactly what he has done (the blasphemy that has horrified the high priest does not move the Roman), tries to get him off by reminding the people that they have, by custom, the right to have a prisoner released at that time, and suggests that he should release Jesus. But they insist on his releasing a prisoner named Barabbas instead, and on having Jesus crucified. Matthew gives no clue to the popularity of Barabbas, describing him simply as "a notable prisoner." The later gospels make it clear, very significantly, that his offence was sedition and insurrection; that he was an advocate of physical force; and that he had killed his man. The choice of Barabbas thus appears as a popular choice of the militant advocate of physical force as against the unresisting advocate of mercy.

THE RESURRECTION

Matthew then tells how after three days an angel opened the family vault of one Joseph, a rich man of Arimathea, who had buried Jesus in it, whereupon Jesus rose and returned from Jerusalem to Galilee and resumed his preaching with his disciples, assuring them that he would now be with them to the end of the world.

At that point the narrative abruptly stops. The story has no ending.

DATE OF MATTHEW'S NARRATIVE

One effect of the promise of Jesus to come again in glory during the lifetime of some of his hearers is to date the gospel without the aid of any scholarship. It must have been written during the lifetime of Jesus's contemporaries: that is, whilst it was still possible for the promise of his Second Coming to be fulfilled. The death of the last person who had been alive when Jesus said "There be some of them that stand here that shall in no wise taste death til they see the Son of Man coming in his kingdom" destroyed the last possibility of the promised Second Coming, and bore out the incredulity of Pilate and the Jews. And as Matthew writes as one believing in that Second Coming, and in fact left his story unfinished to be ended by it, he must have produced his gospel within a lifetime of the crucifixion. Also, he must have believed that reading books would be one of the pleasures of the kingdom of heaven on earth.

CLASS TYPE OF MATTHEW'S JESUS

One more circumstance must be noted as gathered from Matthew. Though he begins his story in such a way as to suggest that Jesus belonged to the privileged classes, he mentions later on that when Jesus attempted to preach in his own country, and had no success there, the people said, "Is not this the carpenter's son?" But Jesus's manner throughout is that of an aristocrat, or at the very least the son of a rich bourgeois, and by no means a lowly-minded one at that. We must be careful therefore to conceive Joseph, not as a modern proletarian carpenter working for weekly wages, but as a master craftsman of royal descent. John the Baptist may have been a Keir Hardie; but the Jesus of Matthew is of the Ruskin-Morris class.

This haughty characterization is so marked that if we had no other documents concerning Jesus than the gospel of Matthew, we should not feel as we do about him. We should have been much less loth to say, "There is a man here who was sane until Peter hailed him as the Christ, and who then became a monomaniac." We should have pointed out that his delusion is a very common delusion among the insane, and that such insanity is quite consistent with the retention of the argumentative cunning and penetration which Jesus displayed in Jerusalem after his delusion had taken complete hold of him. We should feel horrified at the scourging and mocking and crucifixion just as we should if Ruskin had been treated in that way when he also went mad, instead of being cared for as an invalid. And we should have had no clear perception of any special significance in his way of calling the Son of God the Son of Man. We should have noticed that he was a Communist; that he regarded much of what we call law and order as machinery for robbing the poor under legal forms; that he thought domestic ties a snare for the soul; that he agreed with the proverb "The nearer the Church, the farther from God"; that he saw very plainly that the masters of the community should be its servants and not its oppressors and parasites; and that though he did not tell us not to fight our enemies, he did tell us to love them, and warned us that they who draw the sword shall perish by the sword. All this shews a great power of seeing through vulgar illusions, and a capacity for a higher morality than has yet been established in any civilized community; but it does not place Jesus above Confucius or Plato, not to mention more modern philosophers and moralists.

MARK

Let us see whether we can get anything more out of Mark, whose gospel, by the way, is supposed to be older than Matthew's. Mark is brief; and it does not take long to discover that he adds nothing to Matthew except the ending of the story by Christ's ascension into heaven, and the news that many women had come with Jesus to Jerusalem, including Mary Magdalene, out of whom he had cast seven devils. On the other hand Mark says nothing about the birth of Jesus, and does not touch his career until his adult baptism by John. He apparently regards Jesus as a native of Nazareth, as John does, and not of Bethlehem, as Matthew and Luke do, Bethlehem being the city of David, from whom Jesus is said by Matthew and Luke to be descended. He describes John's doctrine as "Baptism of repentance unto remission of sins": that is, a form of Salvationism. He tells us that Jesus went into the synagogues and taught, not as the Scribes but as one having authority: that is, we infer, he preaches his own doctrine as an original moralist instead of repeating what the books say. He describes the miracle of Jesus reaching the boat by walking across the sea, but says nothing about Peter trying to do the same. Mark sees what he relates more vividly than Matthew, and gives touches of detail that bring the event more clearly before the reader. He says, for instance, that when Jesus walked on the waves to the boat, he was passing it by when the disciples called out to him. He seems to feel that Jesus's treatment of the woman of Canaan requires some apology, and therefore says that she was a Greek of Syrophenician race; which probably excused any incivility to her in Mark's eyes. He represents the father of the boy whom Jesus cured of epilepsy after the transfiguration as a sceptic who says "Lord, I believe: help thou mine unbelief." He tells the story of the widow's mite, omitted by Matthew. He explains that Barabbas was "lying bound with them that made in-

surrection, men who in the insurrection had committed murder."
Joseph of Arimathea, who buried Jesus in his own tomb, and
who is described by Matthew as a disciple, is described by Mark
as "one who also himself was looking for the kingdom of God,"
which suggests that he was an independent seeker. Mark earns
our gratitude by making no mention of the old prophecies, and
thereby not only saves time, but avoids the absurd implication
that Christ was merely going through a predetermined ritual, like
the works of a clock, instead of living. Finally Mark reports
Christ as saying, after his resurrection, that those who believe in
him will be saved and those who do not, damned; but it is impossible to discover whether he means anything by a state of
damnation beyond a state of error. The paleographers regard this
passage as tacked on by a later scribe.

On the whole Mark leaves the modern reader where Matthew
left him.

LUKE

LUKE THE LITERARY ARTIST

When we come to Luke, we come to a later story-teller, and
one with a stronger natural gift for his art. Before you have read
twenty lines of Luke's gospel you are aware that you have passed
from the chronicler writing for the sake of recording important
facts, to the artist, telling the story for the sake of telling it. At the
very outset he achieves the most charming idyll in the Bible: the
story of Mary crowded out of the inn into the stable and laying
her newly-born son in the manger, and of the shepherds abiding
in the field keeping watch over their flocks by night, and how the
angel of the Lord came upon them, and the glory of the Lord
shone around them, and suddenly there was with the angel a
multitude of the heavenly host. These shepherds go to the stable
and take the place of the kings in Matthew's chronicle. So completely has this story conquered and fascinated our imagination

that most of us suppose all the gospels to contain it; but it is Luke's story and his alone: none of the others have the smallest hint of it.

THE CHARM OF LUKE'S NARRATIVE

Luke gives the charm of sentimental romance to every incident. The Annunciation, as described by Matthew, is made to Joseph, and is simply a warning to him not to divorce his wife for misconduct. In Luke's gospel it is made to Mary herself, at much greater length, with a sense of the ecstasy of the bride of the Holy Ghost. Jesus is refined and softened almost out of recognition: the stern peremptory disciple of John the Baptist, who never addresses a Pharisee or a Scribe without an insulting epithet, becomes a considerate, gentle, sociable, almost urbane person; and the Chauvinist Jew becomes a pro-Gentile who is thrown out of the synagogue in his own town for reminding the congregation that the prophets had sometimes preferred Gentiles to Jews. In fact they try to throw him down from a sort of Tarpeian rock which they use for executions; but he makes his way through them and escapes: the only suggestion of a feat of arms on his part in the gospels. There is not a word of the Syrophenician woman. At the end he is calmly superior to his sufferings; delivers an address on his way to execution with unruffled composure; does not despair on the cross; and dies with perfect dignity, commending his spirit to God, after praying for the forgiveness of his persecutors on the ground that "They know not what they do." According to Matthew, it is part of the bitterness of his death that even the thieves who are crucified with him revile him. According to Luke, only one of them does this; and he is rebuked by the other, who begs Jesus to remember him when he comes into his kingdom. To which Jesus replies, "This day shalt thou be with me in Paradise," implying that he will spend the three days of his death there. In short, every device is used to get rid of the ruthless horror of the Matthew chronicle, and to relieve the strain of the Passion by touching episodes, and by

33

representing Christ as superior to human suffering. It is Luke's
Jesus who has won our hearts.

THE TOUCH OF PARISIAN ROMANCE

Luke's romantic shrinking from unpleasantness, and his sentimentality, are illustrated by his version of the woman with the
ointment. Matthew and Mark describe it as taking place in the
house of Simon the Leper, where it is objected to as a waste of
money. In Luke's version the leper becomes a rich Pharisee; the
woman becomes a Dame aux Camellias; and nothing is said about
money and the poor. The woman washes the feet of Jesus with
her tears and dries them with her hair; and he is reproached for
suffering a sinful woman to touch him. It is almost an adaptation
of the unromantic Matthew to the Parisian stage. There is a distinct attempt to increase the feminine interest all through. The
slight lead given by Mark is taken up and developed. More is said
about Jesus's mother and her feelings. Christ's following of
women, just mentioned by Mark to account for their presence at
his tomb, is introduced earlier; and some of the women are
named; so that we are introduced to Joanna the wife of Chuza,
Herod's steward, and Susanna. There is the quaint little domestic
episode between Mary and Martha. There is the parable of the
Prodigal Son, appealing to the indulgence romance has always
shewn to Charles Surface and Des Grieux. Women follow Jesus
to the cross; and he makes them a speech beginning "Daughters
of Jerusalem." Slight as these changes may seem, they make a
great change in the atmosphere. The Christ of Matthew could
never have become what is vulgarly called a woman's hero
(though the truth is that the popular demand for sentiment, as
far as it is not simply human, is more manly than womanly); but
the Christ of Luke has made possible those pictures which now
hang in many ladies' chambers, in which Jesus is represented
exactly as he is represented in the Lourdes cinematograph, by a
handsome actor. The only touch of realism which Luke does not

instinctively suppress for the sake of producing this kind of amenity is the reproach addressed to Jesus for sitting down to table without washing his hands; and that is retained because an interesting discourse hangs on it.

WAITING FOR THE MESSIAH

Another new feature in Luke's story is that it begins in a world in which everyone is expecting the advent of the Christ. In Matthew and Mark, Jesus comes into a normal Philistine world like our own of today. Not until the Baptist foretells that one greater than himself shall come after him does the old Jewish hope of a Messiah begin to stir again; and as Jesus begins as a disciple of John, and is baptized by him, nobody connects him with that hope until Peter has the sudden inspiration which produces so startling an effect on Jesus. But in Luke's gospel men's minds, and especially women's minds, are full of eager expectation of a Christ not only before the birth of Jesus, but before the birth of John the Baptist, the event with which Luke begins his story. Whilst Jesus and John are still in their mothers' wombs, John leaps at the approach of Jesus when the two mothers visit one another. At the circumcision of Jesus pious men and women hail the infant as the Christ.

The Baptist himself is not convinced; for at quite a late period in his former disciple's career he sends two young men to ask Jesus is he really the Christ. This is noteworthy because Jesus immediately gives them a deliberate exhibition of miracles, and bids them tell John what they have seen, and ask him what he thinks *now*. This is in complete contradiction to what I have called the Rousseau view of miracles as inferred from Matthew. Luke shews all a romancer's thoughtlessness about miracles: he regards them as "signs": that is, as proofs of the divinity of the person performing them, and not merely of thaumaturgic powers. He revels in miracles just as he revels in parables: they make such capital stories. He cannot allow the calling of Peter, James, and

John from their boats to pass without a comic miraculous over-draft of fishes, with the net sinking the boats and provoking Peter to exclaim, "Depart from me; for I am a sinful man, O Lord," which should probably be translated, "I want no more of your miracles: natural fishing is good enough for my boats."

There are some other novelties in Luke's version. Pilate sends Jesus to Herod, who happens to be in Jerusalem just then, because Herod had expressed some curiosity about him; but nothing comes of it: the prisoner will not speak to him. When Jesus is ill received in a Samaritan village James and John propose to call down fire from heaven and destroy it; and Jesus replies that he is come not to destroy lives but to save them. The bias of Jesus against lawyers is emphasized, and also his resolution not to admit that he is more bound to his relatives than to strangers. He snubs a woman who blesses his mother. As this is contrary to the traditions of sentimental romance, Luke would presumably have avoided it had he not become persuaded that the brotherhood of Man and the Fatherhood of God are superior even to sentimental considerations. The story of the lawyer asking what are the two chief commandments is changed by making Jesus put the question to the lawyer instead of answering it.

As to doctrine, Luke is only clear when his feelings are touched. His logic is weak; for some of the sayings of Jesus are pieced together wrongly, as anyone who has read them in the right order and context in Matthew will discover at once. He does not make anything new out of Christ's mission, and, like the other evangelists, thinks that the whole point of it is that Jesus was the long expected Christ, and that he will presently come back to earth and establish his kingdom, having duly died and risen again after three days. Yet Luke not only records the teaching as to communism and the discarding of hate, which have, of course, nothing to do with the Second Coming, but quotes one very remarkable saying which is not compatible with it, which is, that people must not go about asking where the kingdom of heaven is, and saying "Lo, here!" and "Lo, there!" because the kingdom of heaven is within them. But Luke has no sense that this belongs to a quite different order of thought to his Christianity, and retains undisturbed his view of the kingdom as a locality as definite as Jerusalem or Madagascar.

JOHN

A NEW STORY AND A NEW CHARACTER

The gospel of John is a surprise after the others. Matthew, Mark, and Luke describe the same events in the same order (the variations in Luke are negligible), and their gospels are therefore called the synoptic gospels. They tell substantially the same story of a wandering preacher who at the end of his life came to Jerusalem. John describes a preacher who spent practically his whole adult life in the capital, with occasional visits to the provinces. His circumstantial account of the calling of Peter and the sons of Zebedee is quite different from the others; and he says nothing about their being fishermen. He says expressly that Jesus, though baptized by John, did not himself practise baptism, and that his disciples did. Christ's agonized appeal against his doom in the garden of Gethsemane becomes a cold-blooded suggestion made in the temple at a much earlier period. Jesus argues much more; complains a good deal of the unreasonableness and dislike with which he is met; is by no means silent before Caiaphas and Pilate; lays much greater stress on his resurrection and on the eating of his body (losing all his disciples except the twelve in consequence); says many apparently contradictory and nonsensical things to which no ordinary reader can now find any clue; and gives the impression of an educated, not to say sophisticated mystic, different both in character and schooling from the simple and downright preacher of Matthew and Mark, and the urbane easy-minded charmer of Luke. Indeed, the Jews say of him "How knoweth this man letters, having never learnt?"

ANDROCLES AND THE LION

John the Immortal Eye-Witness

John, moreover, claims to be not only a chronicler but a witness. He declares that he is "the disciple whom Jesus loved," and that he actually leaned on the bosom of Jesus at the last supper and asked in a whisper which of them it was that should betray him. Jesus whispered that he would give a sop to the traitor, and thereupon handed one to Judas, who ate it and immediately became possessed by the devil. This is more natural than the other accounts, in which Jesus openly indicates Judas without eliciting any protest or exciting any comment. It also implies that Jesus deliberately bewitched Judas in order to bring about his own betrayal. Later on John claims that Jesus said to Peter "If I will that John tarry til I come, what is that to thee?"; and John, with a rather obvious mock modesty, adds that he must not claim to be immortal, as the disciples concluded; for Christ did not use that expression, but merely remarked "If I will that he tarry til I come." No other evangelist claims personal intimacy with Christ, or even pretends to be his contemporary (there is no ground for identifying Matthew the publican with Matthew the Evangelist); and John is the only evangelist whose account of Christ's career and character is hopelessly irreconcilable with Matthew's. He is almost as bad as Matthew, by the way, in his repeated explanations of Christ's actions as having no other purpose than to fulfil the old prophecies. The impression is more unpleasant, because, as John, unlike Matthew, is educated, subtle, and obsessed with artificial intellectual mystifications, the discovery that he is stupid or superficial in so simple a matter strikes one with distrust and dislike, in spite of his great literary charm, a good example of which is his transfiguration of the harsh episode of the Syrophenician woman into the pleasant story of the woman of Samaria. This perhaps is why his claim to be John the disciple, or to be a contemporary of Christ or even of any survivor of Christ's generation, has been disputed, and finally, it seems, disallowed. But I repeat, I take no note here of the disputes of experts as to the date of the gospels, not because I am not acquainted with them, but because, as the earliest codices are Greek manuscripts of the fourth century A.D., and the Syrian ones are translations from the Greek, the paleographic expert has no difficulty in arriving at whatever conclusion happens to suit his beliefs or disbeliefs; and he never succeeds in convincing the other experts except when they believe or disbelieve exactly as he does. Hence I conclude that the dates of the original narratives cannot be ascertained, and that we must make the best of the evangelists' own accounts of themselves. There is, as we have seen, a very marked difference between them, leaving no doubt that we are dealing with four authors of well-marked diversity; but they all end in an attitude of expectancy of the Second Coming which they agree in declaring Jesus to have positively and unequivocally promised within the lifetime of his contemporaries. Any believer compiling a gospel after the last of these contemporaries had passed away, would either reject and omit the tradition of that promise on the ground that since it was not fulfilled, and could never now be fulfilled, it could not have been made, or else have had to confess to the Jews, who were the keenest critics of the Christians, that Jesus was either an impostor or the victim of a delusion. Now all the evangelists except Matthew expressly declare themselves to be believers; and Matthew's narrative is obviously not that of a sceptic. I therefore assume as a matter of common sense that, interpolations apart, the gospels are derived from narratives written in the first century A.D. I include John, because though it may be claimed that he hedged his position by claiming that Christ, who specially loved him, endowed him with a miraculous life until the Second Coming, the conclusion being that John is alive at this moment, I cannot believe that a literary forger could hope to save the situation by so outrageous a pretension. Also, John's narrative is in many passages nearer to the realities of public life than the simple chronicle of Matthew or the sentimental romance of Luke. This may be because John was obviously more a man of the world than the others, and knew, as mere chroniclers and romancers never know, what actually happens away from books and desks. But it may also be because he saw and heard what happened instead of collecting traditions about it. The paleographers and daters of first quotations may say what they please: John's claim to give evidence as an eyewitness whilst the others are only compiling history is supported by a certain verisimilitude which appeals to me as one who has preached a new doctrine and argued about it, as well as written stories. This verisimilitude may be dramatic art backed by knowledge of public life; but even at that we must not forget that the best dramatic art is the operation of a divinatory instinct for truth. Be that as it may, John was certainly not the man to believe in the Second Coming and yet give a date for it after that date had passed. There is really no escape from the conclusion that the originals of all the gospels date from the period within which there was still a possibility of the Second Coming occurring at the promised time.

THE PECULIAR THEOLOGY OF JESUS

In spite of the suspicions roused by John's idiosyncrasies, his narrative is of enormous importance to those who go to the gospels for a credible modern religion. For it is John who adds to the other records such sayings as that "I and my father are one"; that "God is a spirit"; that the aim of Jesus is not only that the people should have life, but that they should have it "more abundantly" (a distinction much needed by people who think a man is either alive or dead, and never consider the important question how much alive he is); and that men should bear in mind what they were told in the 82nd Psalm: that they are gods, and are responsible for the doing of the mercy and justice of God. The Jews stoned him for saying these things, and, when he remonstrated with them for stupidly stoning one who had done nothing to them but good works, replied "For a good work we stone thee not; but for blasphemy, because that thou, being a man, makest thyself God." He insists (referring to the 82nd Psalm) that if it is part of their own religion that they are gods on the assurance of God himself, it cannot be blasphemy for him, whom the Father sanctified and sent into the world, to say "I am the son of God." But they will not have this at any price; and he has to escape from their fury. Here the point is obscured by the distinction made by Jesus between himself and other men. He says, in effect, "If you are gods, then, *a fortiori*, I am a god." John makes him say this, just as he makes him say "I am the light of the world." But Matthew makes him say to the people "Ye are the light of the world." John has no grip of the significance of these scraps which he has picked up: he is far more interested in a notion of his own that men can escape death and do even more extraordinary things than Christ himself: in fact, he actually represents Jesus as promising this explicitly, and is finally led into the audacious hint that he, John, is himself immortal in the flesh. Still, he does not miss the significant sayings altogether. However inconsistent they may be with the doctrine he is consciously driving at, they appeal to some sub-intellectual instinct in him that makes him stick them in, like a child sticking tinsel stars on the robe of a toy angel.

John does not mention the ascension; and the end of his narrative leaves Christ restored to life, and appearing from time to time among his disciples. It is on one of these occasions that John describes the miraculous draught of fishes which Luke places at the other end of Christ's career, at the call of the sons of Zebedee.

JOHN AGREED AS TO THE TRIAL AND CRUCIFIXION

Although John, following his practice of shewing Jesus's skill as a debater, makes him play a less passive part at his trial, he still gives substantially the same account of it as all the rest. And the question that would occur to any modern reader never occurs to him, any more than it occurred to Matthew, Mark, or Luke. That question is, Why on earth did not Jesus defend himself, and make the people rescue him from the High Priest? He was so popular that they were unable to prevent him driving the money-changers out of the temple, or to arrest him for it. When they did arrest him afterwards, they had to do it at night in a garden. He could have argued with them as he had often done in the temple, and justified himself both to the Jewish law and to Caesar. And he had physical force at his command to back up his arguments: all that was needed was a speech to rally his followers; and he was not gagged. The reply of the evangelists would have been that all these inquiries are idle, because if Jesus had wished to escape, he could have saved himself all that trouble by doing what John describes him as doing: that is, casting his captors to the earth by an exertion of his miraculous power. If you asked John why he let them get up again and torment and execute him, John would have replied that it was part of the destiny of God to be slain and buried and to rise again, and that to have avoided this destiny would have been to repudiate his Godhead. And that is the only apparent explanation. Whether you believe with the evangelists that Christ could have rescued himself by a miracle, or, as a modern Secularist, point out that he could have defended himself effectually, the fact remains that according to all the narratives he did not do so. He had to die like a god, not to save himself "like one of the princes."[1] The consensus on this point is important, because it proves the absolute sincerity of Jesus's declaration that he was a god. No impostor would have accepted such dreadful consequences without an effort to save himself. No impostor would have been nerved to endure them by the conviction that he would rise from the grave and live again after three days. If we accept the story at all, we must believe this, and

[1] Jesus himself had referred to that psalm (LXXXII) in which men who have judged unjustly and accepted the persons of the wicked (including by anticipation practically all the white inhabitants of the British Isles and the North American continent, to mention no other places) are condemned in the words, "I have said, ye are gods; and all of ye are children of the Most High; but ye shall die like men, and fall like one of the princes."

believe also that his promise to return in glory and establish his kingdom on earth within the lifetime of men then living, was one which he believed that he could, and indeed must fulfil. Two evangelists declare that in his last agony he despaired, and reproached God for forsaking him. The other two represent him as dying in unshaken conviction and charity with the simple remark that the ordeal was finished. But all four testify that his faith was not deceived, and that he actually rose again after three days. And I think it unreasonable to doubt that all four wrote their narratives in full faith that the other promise would be fulfilled too, and that they themselves might live to witness the Second Coming.

CREDIBILITY OF THE GOSPELS

It will be noted by the older among my readers, who are sure to be obsessed more or less by elderly wrangles as to whether the gospels are credible as matter-of-fact narratives, that I have hardly raised this question, and have accepted the credible and incredible with equal complacency. I have done this because credibility is a subjective condition, as the evolution of religious belief clearly shews. Belief is not dependent on evidence and reason. There is as much evidence that the miracles occurred as that the battle of Waterloo occurred, or that a large body of Russian troops passed through England in 1914 to take part in the war on the western front. The reasons for believing in the murder of Pompey are the same as the reasons for believing in the raising of Lazarus. Both have been believed and doubted by men of equal intelligence. Miracles, in the sense of phenomena we cannot explain, surround us on every hand: life itself is the miracle of miracles. Miracles in the sense of events that violate the normal course of our experience are vouched for every day: the flourishing Church of Christ Scientist is founded on a multitude of such miracles. Nobody believes all the miracles: everybody believes some of them. I cannot tell why men who will not

D

believe that Jesus ever existed yet believe firmly that Shakespear was Bacon. I cannot tell why people who believe that angels appeared and fought on our side at the battle of Mons, and who believe that miracles occur quite frequently at Lourdes, nevertheless boggle at the miracle of the liquefaction of the blood of St Januarius, and reject it as a trick of priestcraft. I cannot tell why people who will not believe Matthew's story of three kings bringing costly gifts to the cradle of Jesus, believe Luke's story of the shepherds and the stable. I cannot tell why people, brought up to believe the Bible in the old literal way as an infallible record and revelation, and rejecting that view later on, begin by rejecting the Old Testament, and give up the belief in a brimstone hell before they give up (if they ever do) the belief in a heaven of harps, crowns, and thrones. I cannot tell why people who will not believe in baptism on any terms believe in vaccination with the cruel fanaticism of inquisitors. I am convinced that if a dozen sceptics were to draw up in parallel columns a list of the events narrated in the gospels which they consider credible and incredible respectively, their lists would be different in several particulars. Belief is literally a matter of taste.

FASHIONS IN BELIEF

Now matters of taste are mostly also matters of fashion. We are conscious of a difference between medieval fashions in belief and modern fashions. For instance, though we are more credulous than men were in the Middle Ages, and entertain such crowds of fortune-tellers, magicians, miracle workers, agents of communication with the dead, discoverers of the elixir of life, transmuters of metals, and healers of all sorts, as the Middle Ages never dreamed of as possible, yet we will not take our miracles in the form that convinced the Middle Ages. Arithmetical numbers appealed to the Middle Ages just as they do to us, because they are difficult to deal with, and because the greatest masters of numbers, the Newtons and Leibnitzes, rank among the greatest men.

But there are fashions in numbers too. The Middle Ages took a fancy to some familiar number like seven; and because it was an odd number, and the world was made in seven days, and there are seven stars in Charles's Wain, and for a dozen other reasons, they were ready to believe anything that had a seven or a seven times seven in it. Seven deadly sins, seven swords of sorrow in the heart of the Virgin, seven champions of Christendom, seemed obvious and reasonable things to believe in simply because they were seven. To us, on the contrary, the number seven is the stamp of superstition. We will believe in nothing less than millions. A medieval doctor gained his patient's confidence by telling him that his vitals were being devoured by seven worms. Such a diagnosis would ruin a modern physician. The modern physician tells his patient that he is ill because every drop of his blood is swarming with a million microbes; and the patient believes him abjectly and instantly. Had a bishop told William the Conqueror that the sun was seventy-seven miles distant from the earth, William would have believed him not only out of respect for the Church, but because he would have felt that seventy-seven miles was the proper distance. The Kaiser, knowing just as little about it as the Conqueror, would send that bishop to an asylum. Yet he (I presume) unhesitatingly accepts the estimate of ninety-two and nine-tenths millions of miles, or whatever the latest big figure may be.

CREDIBILITY AND TRUTH

And here I must remind you that our credulity is not to be measured by the truth of the things we believe. When men believed that the earth was flat, they were not credulous: they were using their common sense, and, if asked to prove that the earth was flat, would have said simply, "Look at it." Those who refuse to believe that it is round are exercising a wholesome scepticism. The modern man who believes that the earth is round is grossly credulous. Flat Earth men drive him to fury by confuting him with the greatest ease when he tries to argue about it. Confront him with a theory that the earth is cylindrical, or annular, or hour-glass shaped, and he is lost. The thing he believes may be true, but that is not why he believes it: he believes it because in some mysterious way it appeals to his imagination. If you ask him why he believes that the sun is ninety-odd million miles off, either he will have to confess that he doesnt know, or he will say that Newton proved it. But he has not read the treatise in which Newton proved it, and does not even know that it was written in Latin. If you press an Ulster Protestant as to why he regards Newton as an infallible authority, and St Thomas Aquinas or the Pope as superstitious liars whom, after his death, he will have the pleasure of watching from his place in heaven whilst they roast in eternal flame, or if you ask me why I take into serious consideration Colonel Sir Almroth Wright's estimates of the number of streptococci contained in a given volume of serum whilst I can only laugh at the earlier estimates of the number of angels that can be accommodated on the point of a needle, no reasonable reply is possible except that somehow sevens and angels are out of fashion, and billions and streptococci are all the rage. I simply cannot tell you why Bacon, Montaigne, and Cervantes had a quite different fashion of credulity and incredulity from the Venerable Bede and Piers Plowman and the divine doctors of the Aquinas-Aristotle school, who were certainly no stupider, and had the same facts before them. Still less can I explain why, if we assume that these leaders of thought had all reasoned out their beliefs, their authority seemed conclusive to one generation and blasphemous to another, neither generation having followed the reasoning or gone into the facts of the matter for itself at all.

It is therefore idle to begin disputing with the reader as to what he should believe in the gospels and what he should disbelieve. He will believe what he can, and disbelieve what he must. If he draws any lines at all, they will be quite arbitrary ones. St John tells us that when Jesus explicitly claimed divine honors by the sacrament of his body and blood, so many of his disciples left him that their number was reduced to twelve. Many modern readers will not hold out so long: they will give in at the first miracle. Others will discriminate. They will accept the healing miracles, and reject the feeding of the multitude. To some the walking on the water will be a legendary exaggeration of a swim, ending in an ordinary rescue of Peter; and the raising of Lazarus will be only a similar glorification of a commonplace feat of artificial respiration, whilst others will scoff at it as a planned imposture in which Lazarus acted as a confederate. Between the rejection of the stories as wholly fabulous and the acceptance of them as the evangelists themselves mean them to be accepted, there will be many shades of belief and disbelief, of sympathy and derision. It is not a question of being a Christian or not. A Mahometan Arab will accept literally and without question parts of the narrative which an English Archbishop has to reject or explain away; and many Theosophists and lovers of the wisdom of India, who never enter a Christian Church except as sightseers, will revel in parts of John's gospel which mean nothing to a pious matter-of-fact Bradford manufacturer. Every reader takes from the Bible what he can get. In submitting a précis of the gospel narratives I have not implied any estimate either of their credibility or of their truth. I have simply informed him or reminded him, as the case may be, of what those narratives tell us about their hero.

CHRISTIAN ICONOLATRY AND THE PERIL OF THE ICONOCLAST

I must now abandon this attitude, and make a serious draft on the reader's attention by facing the question whether, if and when the medieval and Methodist will-to-believe the Salvationist and miraculous side of the gospel narratives fails us, as it plainly has failed the leaders of modern thought, there will be anything left of the mission of Jesus: whether, in short, we may not throw the gospels into the waste-paper basket, or put them away on the fiction shelf of our libraries. I venture to reply that we shall be, on the contrary, in the position of the man in Bunyan's riddle who found that "the more he threw away, the more he had." We get rid, to begin with, of the idolatrous or iconographic worship of Christ. By this I mean literally that worship which is given to pictures and statues of him, and to finished and unalterable stories about him. The test of the prevalence of this is that if you speak or write of Jesus as a real live person, or even as a still active God, such worshippers are more horrified than Don Juan was when the statue stepped from its pedestal and came to supper with him. You may deny the divinity of Jesus; you may doubt whether he ever existed; you may reject Christianity for Judaism, Mahometanism, Shintoism, or Fire Worship; and the iconolaters, placidly contemptuous, will only classify you as a freethinker or a heathen. But if you venture to wonder how Christ would have looked if he had shaved and had his hair cut, or what size in shoes he took, or whether he swore when he stood on a nail in the carpenter's shop, or could not button his robe when he was in a hurry, or whether he laughed over the repartees by which he baffled the priests when they tried to trap him into sedition and blasphemy, or even if you tell any part of his story in the vivid terms of modern colloquial slang, you will produce an extraordinary dismay and horror among the iconolaters. You will have made the picture come out of its frame, the statue descend from its pedestal, the story become real, with all the incalculable consequences that may flow from this terrifying miracle. It is at such moments that you realize that the iconolaters have never for a moment conceived Christ as a real person who meant what he said, as a fact, as a force like electricity, only needing the invention of suitable political machinery to be applied to the affairs of mankind with revolutionary effect.

Thus it is not disbelief that is dangerous in our society: it is belief. The moment it strikes you (as it may any day) that Christ is not the lifeless harmless image he has hitherto been to you, but a rallying centre for revolutionary influences which all established States and Churches fight, you must look to yourselves; for you have brought the image to life; and the mob may not be able to bear that horror.

The Alternative to Barabbas

But mobs must be faced if civilization is to be saved. It did not need the present war to shew that neither the iconographic Christ nor the Christ of St Paul has succeeded in effecting the salvation of human society. Whilst I write, the Turks are said to be massacring the Armenian Christians on an unprecedented scale; but Europe is not in a position to remonstrate; for her Christians are slaying one another by every device which civilization has put within their reach as busily as they are slaying the Turks. Barabbas is triumphant everywhere; and the final use he makes of his triumph is to lead us all to suicide with heroic gestures and resounding lies. Now those who, like myself, see the Barabbasque social organization as a failure, and are convinced that the Life Force (or whatever you choose to call it) cannot be finally beaten by any failure, and will even supersede humanity by evolving a higher species if we cannot master the problems raised by the multiplication of our own numbers, have always known that Jesus had a real message, and have felt the fascination of his character and doctrine. Not that we should nowadays dream of claiming any supernatural authority for him, much less the technical authority which attaches to an educated modern philosopher and jurist. But when, having entirely got rid of Salvationist Christianity, and even contracted a prejudice against Jesus on the score of his involuntary connection with it, we engage on a purely scientific study of economics, criminology, and biology, and find that our practical conclusions are virtually those of Jesus, we are distinctly pleased and encouraged to find that we were doing him an injustice, and that the nimbus that surrounds his head in the pictures may be interpreted some day as a light

49

of science rather than a declaration of sentiment or a label of idolatry.

The doctrines in which Jesus is thus confirmed are, roughly, the following:

1. The kingdom of heaven is within you. You are the son of God; and God is the son of man. God is a spirit, to be worshipped in spirit and in truth, and not an elderly gentleman to be bribed and begged from. We are members one of another; so that you cannot injure or help your neighbor without injuring or helping yourself. God is your father: you are here to do God's work; and you and your father are one.

2. Get rid of property by throwing it into the common stock. Dissociate your work entirely from money payments. If you let a child starve you are letting God starve. Get rid of all anxiety about tomorrow's dinner and clothes, because you cannot serve two masters: God and Mammon.

3. Get rid of judges and punishment and revenge. Love your neighbor as yourself, he being a part of yourself. And love your enemies: they are your neighbors.

4. Get rid of your family entanglements. Every mother you meet is as much your mother as the woman who bore you. Every man you meet is as much your brother as the man she bore after you. Dont waste your time at family funerals grieving for your relatives: attend to life, not to death: there are as good fish in the sea as ever came out of it, and better. In the kingdom of heaven, which, as aforesaid, is within you, there is no marriage nor giving in marriage, because you cannot devote your life to two divinities: God and the person you are married to.

Now these are very interesting propositions; and they become more interesting every day, as experience and science drive us more and more to consider them favorably. In considering them, we shall waste our time unless we give them a reasonable construction. We must assume that the man who saw his way through such a mass of popular passion and illusion as stands between us and a sense of the value of such teaching was quite aware of all the objections that occur to an average stockbroker in the first five minutes. It is true that the world is governed to a considerable extent by the considerations that occur to stockbrokers in the first five minutes; but as the result is that the world is so badly governed that those who know the truth can hardly bear to live in it, an objection from an average stockbroker constitutes in itself a *prima facie* case for any social reform.

THE REDUCTION TO MODERN PRACTICE OF CHRISTIANITY

All the same, we must reduce the ethical counsels and proposals of Jesus to modern practice if they are to be of any use to us. If we ask our stockbroker to act simply as Jesus advised his disciples to act, he will reply, very justly, "You are advising me to become a tramp." If we urge a rich man to sell all that he has and give it to the poor, he will inform us that such an operation is impossible. If he sells his shares and his lands, their purchaser will continue all those activities which oppress the poor. If all the rich men take the advice simultaneously the shares will fall to zero and the lands be unsaleable. If one man sells out and throws the money into the slums, the only result will be to add himself and his dependents to the list of the poor, and to do no good to the poor beyond giving a chance few of them a drunken spree. We must therefore bear in mind that whereas, in the time of Jesus, and in the ages which grew darker and darker after his death until the darkness, after a brief false dawn in the Reformation and the Renascence, culminated in the commercial night of the nineteenth century, it was believed that you could not make men good by Act of Parliament, we now know that you cannot make them good in any other way, and that a man who is better than his fellows is a nuisance. The rich man must sell up not only himself but his whole class; and that can be done only through the Chancellor of the Exchequer. The disciple cannot have his bread without money until there is bread for everybody without money; and that requires an elaborate municipal organization of the food supply, rate supported. Being members one of another means One Man One Vote, and One Woman One Vote, and universal suffrage and equal incomes and all sorts of modern political measures. Even in Syria in the time of Jesus his teachings could not possibly have been realized by a series of independent explosions of personal righteousness on the part of the separate units of the population. Jerusalem could not have done what even a village community cannot do, and what Robinson Crusoe himself could not have done if his conscience, and the stern compulsion of Nature, had not imposed a common rule on the half dozen Robinson Crusoes who struggled within him for not wholly compatible satisfactions. And what cannot be done in Jerusalem or Juan Fernandez cannot be done in London, New York, Paris, and Berlin.

In short, Christianity, good or bad, right or wrong, must perforce be left out of the question in human affairs until it is made practically applicable to them by complicated political devices; and to pretend that a field preacher under the governorship of Pontius Pilate, or even Pontius Pilate himself in council with all the wisdom of Rome, could have worked out applications of Christianity or any other system of morals for the twentieth century, is to shelve the subject much more effectually than Nero and all its other persecutors ever succeeded in doing. Personal righteousness, and the view that you cannot make people moral by Act of Parliament, is, in fact, the favorite defensive resort of the people who, consciously or subconsciously, are quite determined not to have their property meddled with by Jesus or any other reformer.

MODERN COMMUNISM

Now let us see what modern experience and sociology have to say to the suggestion of Jesus that you should get rid of your property by throwing it into the common stock. One can hear the Pharisees of Jerusalem and Chorazin and Bethsaida saying, "My good fellow, if you were to divide up the wealth of Judea equally today, before the end of the year you would have rich and poor, poverty and affluence, just as you have today; for there will always be the idle and the industrious, the thrifty and the wasteful, the drunken and the sober; and, as you yourself have very justly observed, the poor we shall have always with us." And we can hear the reply, "Woe unto you, liars and hypocrites; for ye have this very day divided up the wealth of the country yourselves, as must be done every day (for man liveth not otherwise than from hand to mouth, nor can fish and eggs endure for ever); and ye have divided it unjustly; also ye have said that my reproach to you for having the poor always with you was a law unto you that this evil should persist and stink in the nostrils of God to all eternity; wherefore I think that Lazarus will yet see you beside Dives in hell." Modern Capitalism has made short work of the primitive pleas for inequality. The Pharisees themselves have organized communism in capital. Joint stock is the order of the day. An attempt to return to individual properties as the basis of our production would smash civilization more completely than ten revolutions. You cannot get the fields tilled today until the farmer becomes a co-operator. Take the shareholder to his railway, and ask him to point out to you the particular length of rail, the particular seat in the railway carriage, the particular lever in the engine that is his very own and nobody elses; and he will shun you as a madman, very wisely. And if, like Ananias and Sapphira, you try to hold back your little shop or what not from the common stock, represented by the Trust, or Combine, or Kartel, the Trust will presently freeze you out and rope you in and finally strike you dead industrially as thoroughly as St Peter himself. There is no longer any practical question open as to Communism in production: the struggle today is over the distribution of the product: that is, over the daily dividing-up which is the first necessity of organized society.

ANDROCLES AND THE LION

Redistribution

Now it needs no Christ to convince anybody today that our system of distribution is wildly and monstrously wrong. We have million-dollar babies side by side with paupers worn out by a long life of unremitted drudgery. One person in every five dies in a workhouse, a public hospital, or a madhouse. In cities like London the proportion is very nearly one in two. Naturally so outrageous a distribution has to be effected by violence pure and simple. If you demur, you are sold up. If you resist the selling up you are bludgeoned and imprisoned, the process being euphemistically called the maintenance of law and order. Iniquity can go no further. By this time nobody who knows the figures of the distribution defends them. The most bigoted British Conservative hesitates to say that his king should be much poorer than Mr Rockefeller, or to proclaim the moral superiority of prostitution to needlework on the ground that it pays better. The need for a drastic redistribution of income in all civilized countries is now as obvious and as generally admitted as the need for sanitation.

Shall he who Makes, Own?

It is when we come to the question of the proportions in which we are to redistribute that controversy begins. We are bewildered by an absurdly unpractical notion that in some way a man's income should be given to him, not to enable him to live, but as a sort of Sunday School Prize for good behavior. And this folly is complicated by a less ridiculous but quite as unpractical belief that it is possible to assign to each person the exact portion of the national income that he or she has produced. To a child it seems that the blacksmith has made a horse-shoe, and that therefore the horse-shoe is his. But the blacksmith knows that the horse-shoe does not belong solely to him, but to his landlord, to the rate collector and taxgatherer, to the men from whom he bought the iron and anvil and the coals, leaving only a scrap of its value for himself; and this scrap he has to exchange with the butcher and baker and the clothier for the things that he really appropriates as living tissue or its wrappings, paying for all of them more than their cost; for these fellow traders of his have also their landlords and moneylenders to satisfy. If, then, such simple and direct village examples of apparent individual production turn out on a moment's examination to be the products of an elaborate social organization, what is to be said of such products as dreadnoughts, factory-made pins and needles, and steel pens? If God takes the dreadnought in one hand and a steel pen in the other, and asks Job who made them, and to whom they should belong by maker's right, Job must scratch his puzzled head with a potsherd and be dumb, unless indeed it strikes him that God is the ultimate maker, and that all we have a right to do with the product is to feed his lambs.

LABOR TIME

So maker's right as an alternative to taking the advice of Jesus would not work. In practice nothing was possible in that direction but to pay a worker by labor time: so much an hour or day or week or year. But how much? When that question came up, the only answer was "as little as he can be starved into accepting," with the ridiculous results already mentioned, and the additional anomaly that the largest share went to the people who did not work at all, and the least to those who worked hardest. In England nine-tenths of the wealth goes into the pockets of one-tenth of the population.

THE DREAM OF DISTRIBUTION ACCORDING TO MERIT

Against this comes the protest of the Sunday School theorists "Why not distribute according to merit?" Here one imagines Jesus, whose smile has been broadening down the ages as attempt after attempt to escape from his teaching has led to deeper and deeper disaster, laughing outright. Was ever so idiotic a project

ANDROCLES AND THE LION

mooted as the estimation of virtue in money? The London School of Economics is, we must suppose, to set examination papers with such questions as "Taking the money value of the virtues of Jesus as 100, and of Judas Iscariot as zero, give the correct figures for, respectively, Pontius Pilate, the proprietor of the Gadarene swine, the widow who put her mite in the poor-box, Mr Horatio Bottomley, Shakespear, Mr Jack Johnson, Sir Isaac Newton, Palestrina, Offenbach, Sir Thomas Lipton, Mr Paul Cinquevalli, your family doctor, Florence Nightingale, Mrs Siddons, your charwoman, the Archbishop of Canterbury, and the common hangman." Or "The late Mr Barney Barnato received as his lawful income three thousand times as much money as an English agricultural laborer of good general character. Name the principal virtues in which Mr Barnato exceeded the laborer three thousandfold; and give in figures the loss sustained by civilization when Mr Barnato was driven to despair and suicide by the reduction of his multiple to one thousand." The Sunday School idea, with its principle "to each the income he deserves," is really too silly for discussion. Hamlet disposed of it three hundred years ago. "Use every man after his deserts, and who shall scape whipping?" Jesus remains unshaken as the practical man; and we stand exposed as the fools, the blunderers, the unpractical visionaries. The moment you try to reduce the Sunday School idea to figures you find that it brings you back to the hopeless plan of paying for a man's time; and your examination paper will read "The time of Jesus was worth nothing (he complained that the foxes had holes and the birds of the air nests whilst he had not a place to lay his head). Dr Crippen's time was worth, say, three hundred and fifty pounds a year. Criticize this arrangement; and, if you dispute its justice, state in pounds, dollars, francs and marks, what their relative time wages ought to have been." Your answer may be that the question is in extremely bad taste and that you decline to answer it. But you cannot object to being asked how many minutes of a bookmaker's time are worth two hours of an astronomer's?

PREFACE

VITAL DISTRIBUTION

In the end you are forced to ask the question you should have asked at the beginning. What do you give a man an income for? Obviously to keep him alive. Since it is evident that the first condition on which he can be kept alive without enslaving somebody else is that he shall produce an equivalent for what it costs to keep him alive, we may quite rationally compel him to abstain from idling by whatever means we employ to compel him to abstain from murder, arson, forgery, or any other crime. The one supremely foolish thing to do with him is to do nothing: that is to be as idle, lazy, and heartless in dealing with him as he is in dealing with us. Even if we provided work for him instead of basing, as we do, our whole industrial system on successive competitive waves of overwork with their ensuing troughs of unemployment, we should still sternly deny him the alternative of not doing it; for the result must be that he will become poor and make his children poor if he has any; and poor people are cancers in the commonwealth, costing far more than if they were handsomely pensioned off as incurables. Jesus had more sense than to propose anything of the sort. He said to his disciples, in effect, "Do your work for love; and let the other people lodge and feed and clothe you for love." Or, as we should put it nowadays, "for nothing." All human experience and all natural uncommercialized human aspiration point to this as the right path. The Greeks said, "First secure an independent income; and then practise virtue." We all strive towards an independent income. We all know as well as Jesus did that if we have to take thought for the morrow as to whether there shall be anything to eat or drink it will be impossible for us to think of nobler things, or live a higher life than that of a mole, whose life is from beginning to end a frenzied pursuit of food. Until the community is organized in such a way that the fear of bodily want is forgotten as completely as the fear of wolves already is in civilized capitals, we shall never have a decent social life. Indeed the whole attraction of our present arrangement lies in the fact that it does relieve a handful of us from this fear; but as the relief is effected stupidly and wickedly by making the favored handful parasitic on the rest, they are smitten with the degeneracy which seems to be the inevitable biological penalty of complete parasitism. They corrupt culture and statecraft instead of contributing to them, their excessive leisure being as mischievous as the excessive toil of the laborers. Anyhow, the moral is clear. The two main problems of organized society: how to produce subsistence enough for all its members, and how to prevent the theft of that subsistence by idlers, should be carefully dissociated; for the triumphant solution of the first by our inventors and chemists has been offset by the disastrous failure of our rulers to solve the other. Optimism on this point is only wilful blindness: we all have the hard fact of the failure before us. The only people who cling to the lazy delusion that it is possible to find a just distribution that will work automatically are those who postulate some revolutionary change like land nationalization, which by itself would obviously only force into greater urgency the problem of how to distribute the product of the land among all the individuals in the community.

EQUAL DISTRIBUTION

When that problem is at last faced, the question of the proportion in which the national income shall be distributed can have only one answer. All our shares must be equal. It has always been so: it always will be so. It is true that the incomes of robbers vary considerably from individual to individual; and the variation is reflected in the incomes of their parasites. The commercialization of certain exceptional talents has also produced exceptional incomes, direct and derivative. Persons who live on rent of land and capital are economically, though not legally, in the category of robbers, and have grotesquely different incomes. But in the huge mass of mankind variation of income from individual to individual is unknown, because it is ridiculously impracticable.

As a device for persuading a carpenter that a judge is a creature of superior nature to himself, to be deferred and submitted to even to the death, we may give a carpenter a hundred pounds a year and a judge five thousand; but the wage for one carpenter is the wage for all the carpenters: the salary for one judge is the salary for all the judges.

THE CAPTAIN AND THE CABIN BOY

Nothing, therefore, is really in question, or ever has been, but the differences between class incomes. Already there is economic equality between captains, and economic equality between cabin boys. What is at issue still is whether there shall be economic equality between captains and cabin boys. What would Jesus have said? Presumably he would have said that if your only object is to produce a captain and a cabin boy for the purpose of transferring you from Liverpool to New York, or to manoeuvre a fleet and carry powder from the magazine to the gun, then you need give no more than a shilling to the cabin boy for every pound you give to the more expensively trained captain. But if in addition to this you desire to allow the two human souls which are inseparable from the captain and the cabin boy, and which alone differentiate them from the donkey-engine, to develop all their possibilities, then you may find the cabin boy costing rather more than the captain, because cabin boy's work does not do so much for the soul as captain's work. Consequently you will have to give him at least as much as the captain unless you definitely wish him to be a lower creature, in which case the sooner you are hanged as an abortionist the better. That is the fundamental argument.

THE POLITICAL AND BIOLOGICAL OBJECTIONS TO INEQUALITY

But there are other reasons for objecting to class stratification of income which have heaped themselves up since the time of

E

Jesus. In politics it defeats every form of government except that of a necessarily corrupt oligarchy. Democracy in the most democratic modern republics: France and the United States for example, is an imposture and a delusion. It reduces justice and law to a farce: law becomes merely an instrument for keeping the poor in subjection; and accused workmen are tried, not by a jury of their peers, but by conspiracies of their exploiters. The press is the press of the rich and the curse of the poor: it becomes dangerous to teach men to read. The priest becomes the mere complement of the policeman in the machinery by which the countryhouse oppresses the village. Worst of all, marriage becomes a class affair: the infinite variety of choice which nature offers to the young in search of a mate is narrowed to a handful of persons of similar income; and beauty and health become the dreams of artists and the advertisements of quacks instead of the normal conditions of life. Society is not only divided but actually destroyed in all directions by inequality of income between classes: such stability as it has is due to the huge blocks of people between whom there is equality of income.

JESUS AS ECONOMIST

It seems therefore that we must begin by holding the right to an income as sacred and equal, just as we now begin by holding the right to life as sacred and equal. Indeed the one right is only a restatement of the other. To hang me for cutting a dock laborer's throat after making much of me for leaving him to starve when I do not happen to have a ship for him to unload is idiotic; for as he does far less mischief with his throat cut than when he is starving, a rational society would esteem the cutthroat more highly than the capitalist. The thing has become so obvious, and the evil so unendurable, that if our attempt at civilization is not to perish like all the previous ones, we shall have to organize our society in such a way as to be able to say to every person in the land, "Take no thought, saying What shall we eat? or What shall we drink? or Wherewithal shall we be clothed?" We shall then no longer have a race of men whose hearts are in their pockets and safes and at their bankers. As Jesus said, where your treasure is, there will your heart be also. That was why he recommended that money should cease to be a treasure, and that we should take steps to make ourselves utterly reckless of it, setting our minds free for higher uses. In other words, that we should all be gentlemen and take care of our country because our country takes care of us, instead of the commercialized cads we are, doing everything and anything for money, and selling our souls and bodies by the pound and the inch after wasting half the day haggling over the price. Decidedly, whether you think Jesus was God or not, you must admit that he was a first-rate political economist.

Jesus as Biologist

He was also, as we now see, a first-rate biologist. It took a century and a half of evolutionary preachers, from Buffon and Goethe to Butler and Bergson, to convince us that we and our father are one; that as the kingdom of heaven is within us we need not go about looking for it and crying Lo here! and Lo there!; that God is not a picture of a pompous person in white robes in the family Bible, but a spirit; that it is through this spirit that we evolve towards greater abundance of life; that we are the lamps in which the light of the world burns: that, in short, we are gods though we die like men. All that is today sound biology and psychology; and the efforts of Natural Selectionists like Weismann to reduce evolution to mere automatism have not touched the doctrine of Jesus, though they have made short work of the theologians who conceived God as a magnate keeping men and angels as Lord Rothschild keeps buffaloes and emus at Tring.

Money the Midwife of Scientific Communism

It may be asked here by some simple-minded reader why we should not resort to crude Communism as the disciples were told to do. This would be quite practicable in a village where production was limited to the supply of the primitive wants which nature imposes on all human beings alike. We know that people need bread and boots without waiting for them to come and ask for these things and offer to pay for them. But when civilization advances to the point at which articles are produced that no man absolutely needs and that only some men fancy or can use, it is necessary that individuals should be able to have things made to their order and at their own cost. It is safe to provide bread for everybody because everybody wants and eats bread; but it would be absurd to provide microscopes and trombones, pet snakes and polo mallets, alembics and test tubes for everybody, as nine-tenths of them would be wasted; and the nine-tenths of the population who do not use such things would object to their being provided at all. We have in the invaluable instrument called money a means of enabling every individual to order and pay for the particular things he desires over and above the things he must consume in order to remain alive, plus the things the State insists on his having and using whether he wants to or not: for example, clothes, sanitary arrangements, armies and navies. In large communities, where even the most eccentric demands for manufactured articles average themselves out until they can be foreseen within a negligible margin of error, direct communism (Take what you want without payment, as the people do in Morris's News From Nowhere) will, after a little experience, be found not only practicable but highly economical to an extent that now seems impossible. The sportsmen, the musicians, the physicists, the biologists will get their apparatus for the asking as easily as their bread, or, as at present, their paving, street lighting, and bridges; and the deaf man will not object to contribute to communal flutes when the musician has to contribute to communal ear trumpets. There are cases (for example, radium) in which the demand may be limited to the merest handful of laboratory workers, and in which nevertheless the whole community must pay because the price is beyond the means of any individual worker. But even when the utmost allowance is made for extensions of communism that now seem fabulous, there will still remain for a long time to come regions of supply and demand in which men will need and use money or individual credit, and for which, therefore, they must have individual incomes. Foreign travel is an obvious instance. We are so far from even national communism still, that we shall probably have considerable developments of local communism before it becomes possible for a Manchester man to go up to London for a day without taking any money with him. The modern practical form of the communism of Jesus is therefore, for the present, equal distribution of the surplus of the national income that is not absorbed by simple communism.

JUDGE NOT

In dealing with crime and the family, modern thought and experience have thrown no fresh light on the views of Jesus. When Swift had occasion to illustrate the corruption of our civilization by making a catalogue of the types of scoundrels it produces, he always gave judges a conspicuous place alongside of them they judged. And he seems to have done this not as a restatement of the doctrine of Jesus, but as the outcome of his own observation and judgment. One of Mr Gilbert Chesterton's stories has for its hero a judge who, whilst trying a criminal case, is so overwhelmed by the absurdity of his position and the wickedness of the things it forces him to do, that he throws off the ermine there and then, and goes out into the world to live the life of an honest man instead of that of a cruel idol. There has also been a propaganda of a soulless stupidity called Determinism, representing man as a dead object driven hither and thither by his environment, antecedents, circumstances, and so forth, which nevertheless does remind us that there are limits to the number of cubits an individual can add to his stature morally or physically, and that it is silly as well as cruel to torment a man five feet high for not being able to pluck fruit that is within the reach of men of average height. I have known a case of an unfortunate child being beaten for not being able to tell the time after receiving an elaborate explanation of the figures on a clock dial, the fact being that she was short-sighted and could not see them. This is a typical illustration of the absurdities and cruelties into which we are led by the counter-stupidity to Determinism: the doctrine of Free Will. The notion that people can be good if they like, and that you should give them a powerful additional motive for goodness by tormenting them when they do evil, would soon reduce itself to absurdity if its application were not kept within the limits which nature sets to the self-control of most of us. Nobody supposes that a man with no ear for music or no mathematical faculty could be compelled on pain of death, however cruelly inflicted, to hum all the themes of Beethoven's symphonies or to complete Newton's work on fluxions.

LIMITS TO FREE WILL

Consequently such of our laws as are not merely the intimidations by which tyrannies are maintained under pretext of law, can be obeyed through the exercise of a quite common degree of reasoning power and self-control. Most men and women can endure the ordinary annoyances and disappointments of life without committing murderous assaults. They conclude therefore that any person can refrain from such assaults if he or she chooses to, and proceed to reinforce self-control by threats of severe punishment. But in this they are mistaken. There are people, some of them possessing considerable powers of mind and body, who can no more restrain the fury into which a trifling mishap throws them than a dog can restrain himself from snapping if he is suddenly and painfully pinched. People fling knives and lighted paraffin lamps at one another in a dispute over a dinner-table. Men who have suffered several long sentences of penal servitude for murderous assaults will, the very day after they are released, seize their wives and cast them under drays at an irritating word. We have not only people who cannot resist an opportunity of stealing for the sake of satisfying their wants, but even people who have a specific mania for stealing, and do it when they are in no need of the things they steal. Burglary fascinates some men as sailoring fascinates some boys. Among respectable people how many are there who can be restrained by the warnings of their doctors and the lessons of experience from eating and drinking more than is good for them? It is true that between self-controlled people and ungovernable people there is a narrow margin of moral malingerers who can be made to behave themselves by the fear of consequences; but it is not worth while maintaining an abominable system of malicious, deliberate, costly and degrading ill-treatment of criminals for the sake of these marginal cases. For practical dealing with crime, Determinism or Predestination is quite a good working rule. People without self-control enough for social purposes may be killed, or may be kept in asylums with a view to studying their condition and ascertaining whether it is curable. To torture them and give ourselves virtuous airs at their expense is ridiculous and barbarous; and the desire to do it is vindictive and cruel. And though vindictiveness and cruelty are at least human qualities when they are frankly proclaimed and indulged, they are loathsome when they assume the robes of Justice. Which, I take it, is why Shakespear's Isabella gave such a dressing-down to Judge Angelo, and why Swift reserved the hottest corner of his hell for judges. Also, of course, why Jesus said "Judge not that ye be not judged" and "If any man hear my words and believe not, I judge him not" because "he hath one that judgeth him": namely, the Father who is one with him.

When we are robbed we generally appeal to the criminal law, not considering that if the criminal law were effective we should not have been robbed. That convicts us of vengeance.

I need not elaborate the argument further. I have dealt with it sufficiently elsewhere. I have only to point out that we have been judging and punishing ever since Jesus told us not to; and I defy anyone to make out a convincing case for believing that the world has been any better than it would have been if there had never been a judge, a prison, or a gallows in it all that time. We have simply added the misery of punishment to the misery of crime, and the cruelty of the judge to the cruelty of the criminal. We have taken the bad man, and made him worse by torture and degradation, incidentally making ourselves worse in the process. It does not seem very sensible, does it? It would have been far easier to kill him as kindly as possible, or to label him and leave him to his conscience, or to treat him as an invalid or a lunatic is now treated (it is only of late years, by the way, that madmen have been delivered from the whip, the chain, and the cage); and this, I presume, is the form in which the teaching of Jesus could have been put into practice.

JESUS ON MARRIAGE AND THE FAMILY

When we come to marriage and the family, we find Jesus making the same objection to that individual appropriation of human beings which is the essence of matrimony as to the individual appropriation of wealth. A married man, he said, will try to please his wife, and a married woman to please her husband, instead of doing the work of God. This is another version of "Where your treasure is, there will your heart be also." Eighteen hundred years later we find a very different person from Jesus, Talleyrand to wit, saying the same thing. A married man with a family, said Talleyrand, will do anything for money. Now this, though not a scientifically precise statement, is true enough to be a moral objection to marriage. As long as a man has a right to risk his life or his livelihood for his ideas he needs only courage and conviction to make his integrity unassailable. But he forfeits that right when he marries. It took a revolution to rescue Wagner from his Court appointment at Dresden; and his wife never forgave him for being glad and feeling free when he lost it and threw her back into poverty. Millet might have gone on painting potboiling nudes to the end of his life if his wife had not been of a heroic turn herself. Women, for the sake of their children and parents, submit to slaveries and prostitutions that no unattached woman would endure.

This was the beginning and the end of the objection of Jesus to marriage and family ties, and the explanation of his conception of heaven as a place where there should be neither marrying nor giving in marriage. Now there is no reason to suppose that when he said this he did not mean it. He did not, as St Paul did afterwards in his name, propose celibacy as a rule of life; for he was not a fool, nor, when he denounced marriage, had he yet come to believe, as St Paul did, that the end of the world was at hand and there was therefore no more need to replenish the earth. He must have meant that the race should be continued without dividing with women and men the allegiance the individual owes to God within him. This raises the practical problem of how we are to secure the spiritual freedom and integrity of the priest and the nun without their barrenness and uncompleted experience. Luther the priest did not solve the problem by marrying a nun: he only testified in the most convincing and practical way to the fact that celibacy was a worse failure than marriage.

WHY JESUS DID NOT MARRY

To all appearance the problem oppresses only a few exceptional people. Thoroughly conventional women married to thoroughly conventional men should not be conscious of any restriction: the chain not only leaves them free to do whatever they want to do, but greatly facilitates their doing it. To them an attack on marriage is not a blow struck in defence of their freedom but at their rights and privileges. One would expect that they would not only demur vehemently to the teachings of Jesus in this matter, but object strongly to his not having been a married man himself. Even those who regard him as a god descended from his throne in heaven to take on humanity for a time might reasonably declare that the assumption of humanity must have been incomplete at its most vital point if he were a celibate. But the facts are flatly contrary. The mere thought of Jesus as a married man is felt to be blasphemous by the most conventional believers; and even those of us to whom Jesus is no supernatural personage, but a prophet only as Mahomet was a prophet, feel that there was something more dignified in the bachelordom of Jesus than in the spectacle of Mahomet lying distracted on the floor of his harem whilst his wives stormed and squabbled and henpecked round him. We are not surprised that when Jesus called the sons of Zebedee to follow him, he did not call their father, and that the disciples, like Jesus himself, were all men without family entanglements. It is evident from his impatience when people excused themselves from following him because of their family funerals, or when they assumed that his first duty was to his mother, that he had found family ties and domestic affections in his way at every turn, and had become persuaded at last that no man could follow his inner light until he was free from their compulsion. The absence of any protest against this tempts us to declare that on this question of marriage there are no conventional people; and that everyone of us is at heart a good Christian sexually.

INCONSISTENCY OF THE SEX INSTINCT

But the question is not so simple as that. Sex is an exceedingly subtle and complicated instinct; and the mass of mankind neither know nor care much about freedom of conscience, which is what Jesus was thinking about, and are concerned almost to obsession with sex, as to which Jesus said nothing. In our sexual natures we are torn by an irresistible attraction and an overwhelming repugnance and disgust. We have two tyrannous physical passions: concupiscence and chastity. We become mad in pursuit of sex: we become equally mad in the persecution of that pursuit. Unless we gratify our desire the race is lost: unless we restrain it we destroy ourselves. We are thus led to devise marriage institutions which will at the same time secure opportunities for the gratification of sex and raise up innumerable obstacles to it; which will sanctify it and brand it as infamous; which will identify it with virtue and with sin simultaneously. Obviously it is useless to look for any consistency in such institutions; and it is only by continual reform and readjustment, and by a considerable elasticity in their enforcement, that a tolerable result can be arrived at. I need not repeat here the long and elaborate examination of them that I prefixed to my play entitled Getting Married. Here I am concerned only with the views of Jesus on the question; and it is necessary, in order to understand the attitude of the world towards them, that we should not attribute the general approval of the decision of Jesus to remain unmarried as an endorsement of his views. We are simply in a state of confusion on the subject; but it is part of the confusion that we should conclude that Jesus was a celibate, and shrink even from the idea that his birth was a natural one, yet cling with ferocity to the sacredness of the institution which provides a refuge from celibacy.

For Better for Worse

Jesus, however, did not express a complicated view of marriage. His objection to it was quite simple, as we have seen. He perceived that nobody could live the higher life unless money and sexual love were obtainable without sacrificing it; and he saw that the effect of marriage as it existed among the Jews (and as it still exists among ourselves) was to make the couples sacrifice every higher consideration until they had fed and pleased one another. The worst of it is that this dangerous preposterousness in marriage, instead of improving as the general conduct of married couples improves, becomes much worse. The selfish man to whom his wife is nothing but a slave, the selfish woman to whom her husband is nothing but a scapegoat and a breadwinner, are not held back from spiritual or any other adventures by fear of their effect on the welfare of their mates. Their wives do not make recreants and cowards of them: their husbands do not chain them to the cradle and the cooking range when their feet should be beautiful on the mountains. It is precisely as people become more kindly, more conscientious, more ready to shoulder the heavier part of the burden (which means that the strong shall give way to the weak and the slow hold back the swift), that marriage becomes an intolerable obstacle to individual evolution. And that is why the revolt against marriage of which Jesus was an exponent always recurs when civilization raises the standard of marital duty and affection, and at the same time produces a greater need for individual freedom in pursuit of a higher evolution.

THE REMEDY

This, fortunately, is only one side of marriage; and the question arises, can it not be eliminated? The reply is reassuring: of course it can. There is no mortal reason in the nature of things why a married couple should be economically dependent on one another. The Communism advocated by Jesus, which we have seen to be entirely practicable, and indeed inevitable if our civilization is to be saved from collapse, gets rid of that difficulty completely. And with the economic dependence will go the force of the outrageous claims that derive their real sanction from the economic pressure behind them. When a man allows his wife to turn him from the best work he is capable of doing, and to sell his soul at the highest commercial prices obtainable; when he allows her to entangle him in a social routine that is wearisome and debilitating to him, or tie him to her apron strings when he needs that occasional solitude which is one of the most sacred of human rights, he does so because he has no right to impose eccentric standards of expenditure and unsocial habits on her, and because these conditions have produced by their pressure so general a custom of chaining wedded couples to one another that married people are coarsely derided when their partners break the chain. And when a woman is condemned by her parents to wait in genteel idleness and uselessness for a husband when all her healthy social instincts call her to acquire a profession and work, it is again her economic dependence on them that makes their tyranny effective.

The Case for Marriage

Thus, though it would be too much to say that everything that is obnoxious in marriage and family life will be cured by Communism, yet it can be said that it will cure what Jesus objected to in these institutions. He made no comprehensive study of them: he only expressed his own grievance with an overwhelming sense that it is a grievance so deep that all the considerations on the other side are as dust in the balance. Obviously there are such considerations, and very weighty ones too. When Talleyrand said that a married man with a family is capable of anything, he meant anything evil; but an optimist may declare, with equal half truth, that a married man is capable of anything good; that marriage turns vagabonds into steady citizens; and that men and women will, for love of their mates and children, practise virtues that unattached individuals are incapable of. It is true that too much of this domestic virtue is self-denial, which is not a virtue at all; but then the following of the inner light at all costs is largely self-indulgence, which is just as suicidal, just as weak, just as cowardly as self-denial. Ibsen, who takes us into the matter far more resolutely than Jesus, is unable to find any golden rule: both Brand and Peer Gynt come to a bad end; and though Brand does not do as much mischief as Peer, the mischief he does do is of extraordinary intensity.

Celibacy no Remedy

We must, I think, regard the protest of Jesus against marriage and family ties as the claim of a particular kind of individual to be free from them because they hamper his own work intolerably. When he said that if we are to follow him in the sense of taking up his work we must give up our family ties, he was simply stating a fact; and to this day the Roman Catholic priest, the Buddhist lama, and the fakirs of all the eastern denominations accept the saying. It is also accepted by the physically enterprising, the explorers, the restlessly energetic of all kinds: in short, by the adventurous. The greatest sacrifice in marriage is the sacrifice of the adventurous attitude towards life: the being settled. Those who are born tired may crave for settlement; but to fresher and stronger spirits it is a form of suicide.

Now to say of any institution that it is incompatible with both the contemplative and adventurous life is to disgrace it so vitally that all the moralizings of all the Deans and Chapters cannot reconcile our souls to its slavery. The unmarried Jesus and the unmarried Beethoven, the unmarried Joan of Arc, Clare, Teresa, Florence Nightingale seem as they should be; and the saying that there is always something ridiculous about a married philosopher becomes inevitable. And yet the celibate is still more ridiculous than the married man: the priest, in accepting the alternative of celibacy, disables himself; and the best priests are those who have been men of this world before they became men of the world to come. But as the taking of vows does not annul an existing marriage, and a married man cannot become a priest, we are again confronted with the absurdity that the best priest is a reformed rake. Thus does marriage, itself intolerable, thrust us upon intolerable alternatives. The practical solution is to make the individual economically independent of marriage and the family, and to make marriage as easily dissoluble as any other partnership: in other words, to accept the conclusions to which experience is slowly driving both our sociologists and our legislators. This will not instantly cure all the evils of marriage, nor root up at one stroke its detestable tradition of property in human bodies. But it will leave Nature free to effect a cure; and in free soil the root may wither and perish.

This disposes of all the opinions and teachings of Jesus which are still matters of controversy. They are all in line with the best modern thought. He told us what we have to do; and we have had to find the way to do it. Most of us are still, as most were in his own time, extremely recalcitrant, and are being forced along that way by painful pressure of circumstances, protesting at every step that nothing will induce us to go; that is a ridiculous way, a disgraceful way, a socialistic way, an atheistic way, an immoral way, and that the vanguard ought to be ashamed of themselves and must be made to turn back at once. But they find that they have to follow the vanguard all the same if their lives are to be worth living.

AFTER THE CRUCIFIXION

Let us now return to the New Testament narrative; for what happened after the disappearance of Jesus is instructive. Unfortunately, the crucifixion was a complete political success. I remember that when I described it in these terms once before, I greatly shocked a most respectable newspaper in my native town, the Dublin Daily Express, because my journalistic phrase shewed that I was treating it as an ordinary event like Home Rule or the Insurance Act: that is (though this did not occur to the editor), as a real event which had really happened, instead of a portion of the Church service. I can only repeat, assuming as I am that it *was* a real event and did actually happen, that it was as complete a success as any in history. Christianity as a specific doctrine was slain with Jesus, suddenly and utterly. He was hardly cold in his grave, or high in his heaven (as you please), before the apostles dragged the tradition of him down to the level of the thing it has remained ever since. And that thing the intelligent heathen may study, if they would be instructed in it by modern books, in Samuel Butler's novel, The Way of All Flesh.

The Vindictive Miracles and the Stoning of Stephen

Take, for example, the miracles. Of Jesus alone of all the Christian miracle workers there is no record, except in certain gospels that all men reject, of a malicious or destructive miracle. A barren fig-tree was the only victim of his anger. Every one of his miracles on sentient subjects was an act of kindness. John declares that he healed the wound of the man whose ear was cut off (by Peter, John says) at the arrest in the garden. One of the first things the apostles did with their miraculous power was to strike dead a wretched man and his wife who had defrauded them by holding back some money from the common stock. They struck people blind or dead without remorse, judging because they had been judged. They healed the sick and raised the dead apparently in a spirit of pure display and advertisement. Their doctrine did not contain a ray of that light which reveals Jesus as one of the redeemers of men from folly and error. They cancelled him, and went back straight to John the Baptist and his formula of securing remission of sins by repentance and the rite of baptism (being born again of water and the spirit). Peter's first harangue softens us by the human touch of its exordium, which was a quaint assurance to his hearers that they must believe him to be sober because it was too early in the day to get drunk; but of Jesus he had nothing to say except that he was the Christ foretold by the prophets as coming from the seed of David, and that they must believe this and be baptized. To this the other apostles added incessant denunciations of the Jews for having crucified him, and threats of the destruction that would overtake them if they did not repent: that is, if they did not join the sect which the apostles were now forming. A quite intolerable young speaker named Stephen delivered an oration to the council, in which he first inflicted on them a tedious sketch of the history of Israel, with which they were presumably as well acquainted as he, and then reviled them in the most insulting terms as "stiffnecked and uncircumcized." Finally, after boring and annoying them to the utmost bearable extremity, he looked up and declared that he saw the heavens open, and Christ standing on the right hand of God. This was too much: they threw him out of the city and stoned him to death. It was a severe way of suppressing a tactless and conceited bore; but it was pardonable and human in comparison to the slaughter of poor Ananias and Sapphira.

PAUL

Suddenly a man of genius, Paul, violently anti-Christian, enters on the scene, holding the clothes of the men who are stoning Stephen. He persecutes the Christians with great vigor, a sport which he combines with the business of a tentmaker. This temperamental hatred of Jesus, whom he has never seen, is a pathological symptom of that particular sort of conscience and nervous constitution which brings its victims under the tyranny of two delirious terrors: the terror of sin and the terror of death, which may be called also the terror of sex and the terror of life. Now Jesus, with his healthy conscience on his higher plane, was free from these terrors. He consorted freely with sinners, and was never concerned for a moment, as far as we know, about whether his conduct was sinful or not; so that he has forced us to accept him as the man without sin. Even if we reckon his last days as the days of his delusion, he none the less gave a fairly convincing exhibition of superiority to the fear of death. This must have both fascinated and horrified Paul, or Saul, as he was first called. The horror accounts for his fierce persecution of the Christians. The fascination accounts for the strangest of his fancies: the fancy for attaching the name of Jesus Christ to the great idea which flashed upon him on the road to Damascus, the idea that he could not only make a religion of his two terrors, but that the movement started by Jesus offered him the nucleus for his new Church. It

F

was a monstrous idea; and the shock of it, as he afterwards declared, struck him blind for days. He heard Jesus calling to him from the clouds, "Why persecute me?" His natural hatred of the teacher for whom Sin and Death had no terrors turned into a wild personal worship of him which has the ghastliness of a beautiful thing seen in a false light.

The chronicler of the Acts of the Apostles sees nothing of the significance of this. The great danger of conversion in all ages has been that when the religion of the high mind is offered to the lower mind, the lower mind, feeling its fascination without understanding it, and being incapable of rising to it, drags it down to its level by degrading it. Years ago I said that the conversion of a savage to Christianity is the conversion of Christianity to savagery. The conversion of Paul was no conversion at all: it was Paul who converted the religion that has raised one man above sin and death into a religion that delivered millions of men so completely into their dominion that their own common nature became a horror to them, and the religious life became a denial of life. Paul had no intention of surrendering either his Judaism or his Roman citizenship to the new moral world (as Robert Owen called it) of Communism and Jesuism. Just as in our own time Karl Marx, not content to take political economy as he found it, insisted on rebuilding it from the bottom upwards in his own way, and thereby gave a new lease of life to the errors it was just outgrowing, so Paul reconstructed the old Salvationism from which Jesus had vainly tried to redeem him, and produced a fantastic theology which is still the most amazing thing of the kind known to us. Being intellectually an inveterate Roman Rationalist, always discarding the irrational real thing for the unreal but ratiocinable postulate, he began by discarding Man as he is, and substituted a postulate which he called Adam. And when he was asked, as he surely must have been in a world not wholly mad, what had become of the natural man, he replied "Adam *is* the natural man." This was confusing to simpletons, because according to tradition Adam was certainly the name of the natural man as created in the garden of Eden. It was as if a preacher of our own time had described as typically British Frankenstein's monster, and called him Smith, and somebody, on demanding what about the man in the street, had been told "Smith *is* the man in the street." The thing happens often enough; for indeed the world is full of these Adams and Smiths and men in the street and average sensual men and economic men and womanly women and what not, all of them imaginary Atlases carrying imaginary worlds on their unsubstantial shoulders.

The Eden story provided Adam with a sin: the "original sin" for which we are all damned. Baldly stated, this seems ridiculous; nevertheless it corresponds to something actually existent not only in Paul's consciousness but in our own. The original sin was not the eating of the forbidden fruit, but the consciousness of sin which the fruit produced. The moment Adam and Eve tasted the apple they found themselves ashamed of their sexual relation, which until then had seemed quite innocent to them; and there is no getting over the hard fact that this shame, or state of sin, has persisted to this day, and is one of the strongest of our instincts. Thus Paul's postulate of Adam as the natural man was pragmatically true: it worked. But the weakness of Pragmatism is that most theories will work if you put your back into making them work, provided they have some point of contact with human nature. Hedonism will pass the pragmatic test as well as Stoicism. Up to a certain point every social principle that is not absolutely idiotic works: Autocracy works in Russia and Democracy in America; Atheism works in France, Polytheism in India, Monotheism throughout Islam, and Pragmatism, or No-ism, in England. Paul's fantastic conception of the damned Adam, represented by Bunyan as a pilgrim with a great burden of sins on his back, corresponded to the fundamental condition of evolution, which is, that life, including human life, is continually evolving, and must therefore be continually ashamed of itself and its present and past. Bunyan's pilgrim wants to get rid of his bundle of sins; but he also wants to reach "yonder shining light"; and when at last his bundle falls off him into the sepulchre of Christ, his pilgrimage is still unfinished and his hardest trials still ahead of him. His conscience remains uneasy; "original sin" still torments him; and his adventure with Giant Despair, who throws him into the dungeon of Doubting Castle, from which he escapes by the use of a skeleton key, is more terrible than any he met whilst the bundle was still on his back. Thus Bunyan's allegory of human nature breaks through the Pauline theology at a hundred points. His theological allegory, The Holy War, with its troops of Election Doubters, and its cavalry of "those that rode Reformadoes," is, as a whole, absurd, impossible, and, except in passages where the artistic old Adam momentarily got the better of the Salvationist theologian, hardly readable.

Paul's theory of original sin was to some extent idiosyncratic. He tells us definitely that he finds himself quite well able to avoid the sinfulness of sex by practising celibacy; but he recognizes, rather contemptuously, that in this respect he is not as other men are, and says that they had better marry than burn, thus admitting that though marriage may lead to placing the desire to please wife or husband before the desire to please God, yet preoccupation with unsatisfied desire may be even more ungodly than preoccupation with domestic affection. This view of the case inevitably led him to insist that a wife should be rather a slave than a partner, her real function being, not to engage a man's love and loyalty, but on the contrary to release them for God by relieving the man of all preoccupation with sex just as in her capacity of housekeeper and cook she relieves his preoccupation with hunger by the simple expedient of satisfying his appetite. This slavery also justifies itself pragmatically by working effectively; but it has made Paul the eternal enemy of Woman. Incidentally it has led to many foolish surmises about Paul's personal character and circumstances, by people so enslaved by sex that a celibate appears to them a sort of monster. They forget that not only whole priesthoods, official and unofficial, from Paul to Carlyle and Ruskin, have defied the tyranny of sex, but immense numbers of ordinary citizens of both sexes have, either voluntarily or under pressure of circumstances easily surmountable, saved their energies for less primitive activities.

Howbeit, Paul succeeded in stealing the image of Christ crucified for the figure-head of his Salvationist vessel, with its Adam posing as the natural man, its doctrine of original sin, and its damnation avoidable only by faith in the sacrifice of the cross. In fact, no sooner had Jesus knocked over the dragon of superstition than Paul boldly set it on its legs again in the name of Jesus.

THE CONFUSION OF CHRISTENDOM

Now it is evident that two religions having such contrary effects on mankind should not be confused as they are under a common name. There is not one word of Pauline Christianity in the characteristic utterances of Jesus. When Saul watched the clothes of the men who stoned Stephen, he was not acting upon beliefs which Paul renounced. There is no record of Christ's having ever said to any man: "Go and sin as much as you like: you can put it all on me." He said "Sin no more," and insisted that he was putting up the standard of conduct, not debasing it, and that the righteousness of the Christian must exceed that of the Scribe and Pharisee. The notion that he was shedding his blood in order that every petty cheat and adulterator and libertine might wallow in it and come out whiter than snow, cannot be imputed to him on his own authority. "I come as an infallible patent medicine for bad consciences" is not one of the sayings in the gospels. If Jesus could have been consulted on Bunyan's allegory as to that business of the burden of sin dropping from the pilgrim's back when he caught sight of the cross, we must infer from his teaching that he would have told Bunyan in forcible terms that he had never made a greater mistake in his life, and that the business of a Christ was to make self-satisfied sinners feel the burden of their sins and stop committing them instead of assuring them that they could not help it, as it was all Adam's fault, but that it did not matter as long as they were credulous and friendly about himself. Even when he believed himself to be a god, he did not regard himself as a scapegoat. He was to take away the sins of the world by good government, by justice and mercy, by setting the welfare of little children above the pride of princes, by casting all the quackeries and idolatries which now usurp and malversate the power of God into what our local authorities quaintly call the dust destructor, and by riding on the clouds of heaven in glory instead of in a thousand-guinea motor car. That was delirious, if you like; but it was the delirium of a free soul, not of a shame-bound one like Paul's. There has really never been a more monstrous imposition perpetrated than the imposition of the limitations of Paul's soul upon the soul of Jesus.

THE SECRET OF PAUL'S SUCCESS

Paul must soon have found that his followers had gained peace of mind and victory over death and sin at the cost of all moral responsibility; for he did his best to reintroduce it by making good conduct the test of sincere belief, and insisting that sincere belief was necessary to salvation. But as his system was rooted in the plain fact that as what he called sin includes sex and is therefore an ineradicable part of human nature (why else should Christ have had to atone for the sin of all future generations?) it was impossible for him to declare that sin, even in its wickedest extremity, could forfeit the sinner's salvation if he repented and believed. And to this day Pauline Christianity is, and owes its enormous vogue to being, a premium on sin. Its consequences have had to be held in check by the worldlywise majority through a violently anti-Christian system of criminal law and stern morality. But of course the main restraint is human nature, which has good impulses as well as bad ones, and refrains from theft and murder and cruelty, even when it is taught that it can commit them all at the expense of Christ and go happily to heaven afterwards, simply because it does not always want to murder or rob or torture.

It is now easy to understand why the Christianity of Jesus failed completely to establish itself politically and socially, and was easily suppressed by the police and the Church, whilst Paulinism overran the whole western civilized world, which was at that time the Roman Empire, and was adopted by it as its official faith, the old avenging gods falling helplessly before the new Redeemer. It still retains, as we may see in Africa, its power of bringing to simple people a message of hope and consolation that no other religion offers. But this enchantment is produced by its spurious association with the personal charm of Jesus, and exists only for untrained minds. In the hands of a logical Frenchman like Calvin, pushing it to its utmost conclusions, and devising "institutes" for hardheaded adult Scots and literal Swiss, it becomes the most infernal of fatalisms; and the lives of civilized children are blighted by its logic whilst negro piccaninnies are rejoicing in its legends.

PAUL'S QUALITIES

Paul, however, did not get his great reputation by mere imposition and reaction. It is only in comparison with Jesus (to whom many prefer him) that he appears common and conceited. Though in The Acts he is only a vulgar revivalist, he comes out in his own epistles as a genuine poet, though by flashes only. He is no more a Christian than Jesus was a Baptist: he is a disciple of Jesus only as Jesus was a disciple of John. He does nothing that Jesus would have done, and says nothing that Jesus would have said, though much, like the famous ode to charity, that he would have admired. He is more Jewish than the Jews, more Roman than the Romans, proud both ways, full of startling confessions and self-revelations that would not surprise us if they were slipped into the pages of Nietzsche, tormented by an intellectual conscience that demanded an argued case even at the cost of sophistry, with all sorts of fine qualities and occasional illuminations, but always hopelessly in the toils of Sin, Death, and Logic, which had no power over Jesus. As we have seen, it was by introducing this bondage and terror of his into the Christian doctrine that he adapted it to the Church and State systems which Jesus transcended, and made it practicable by destroying the specifically Jesuist side of it. He would have been quite in his place in any modern Protestant State; and he, not Jesus, is the true head and founder of our Reformed Church, as Peter is of the Roman Church. The followers of Paul and Peter made Christendom, whilst the Nazarenes were wiped out.

THE ACTS OF THE APOSTLES

Here we may return to the narrative called The Acts of the Apostles, which we left at the point where the stoning of Stephen was followed by the introduction of Paul. The author of The Acts, though a good story-teller, like Luke, was (herein also like Luke) much weaker in power of thought than in imaginative literary art. Hence we find Luke credited with the authorship of The Acts by people who like stories and have no aptitude for theology, whilst the book itself is denounced as spurious by Pauline theologians because Paul, and indeed all the apostles, are represented in it as very commonplace revivalists, interesting us by their adventures more than by any qualities of mind or character. Indeed, but for the epistles, we should have a very poor opinion of the apostles. Paul in particular is described as setting a fashion which has remained in continual use to this day. Whenever he addresses an audience, he dwells with great zest on his misdeeds before his pseudo conversion, with the effect of throwing into stronger relief his present state of blessedness; and he tells the story of that conversion over and over again, ending with exhortations to the hearers to come and be saved, and threats of the wrath that will overtake them if they refuse. At any revival meeting today the same thing may be heard, followed by the same conversions. This is natural enough; but it is totally unlike the preaching of Jesus, who never talked about his personal history, and never "worked up" an audience to hysteria. It aims at a purely nervous effect; it brings no enlightenment; the most ignorant man has only to become intoxicated with his own vanity, and mistake his self-satisfaction for the Holy Ghost, to become qualified as an apostle; and it has absolutely nothing to do with the characteristic doctrines of Jesus. The Holy Ghost may be at work all round producing wonders of art and science, and strengthening men to endure all sorts of martyrdoms for the enlargement of knowledge, and the enrichment and intensification of life ("that ye may have life more abundantly"); but the apostles, as described in The Acts, take no part in the struggle except as persecutors and revilers. To this day, when their successors get the upper hand, as in Geneva (Knox's "perfect city of Christ") and in Scotland and Ulster, every spiritual activity but moneymaking and churchgoing is stamped out; heretics are ruthlessly persecuted; and such pleasures as money can purchase are suppressed so that its possessors are compelled to go on making money because there is nothing else to do. And the compensation for all this privation is partly an insane conceit of being the elect of God, with a reserved seat in heaven, and partly, since even the most infatuated idiot cannot spend his life admiring himself, the less innocent excitement of punishing other people for not admiring him, and the nosing out of the sins of the people who, being intelligent enough to be incapable of mere dull self-righteousness, and highly susceptible to the beauty and interest of the real workings of the Holy Ghost, try to live more rational and abundant lives. The abominable amusement of terrifying children with threats of hell is another of these diversions, and perhaps the vilest and most mischievous of them. The net result is that the imitators of the apostles, whether they are called Holy Willies or Stigginses in derision, or, in admiration, Puritans or saints, are, outside their own congregations, and to a considerable extent inside them, heartily detested. Now nobody detests Jesus, though many who have been tormented in their childhood in his name include him in their general loathing of everything connected with the word religion; whilst others, who know him only by misrepresentation as a sentimental pacifist and an ascetic, include him in their general dislike of that type of character. In the same way a student who has had to "get up" Shakespear as a college subject may hate Shakespear; and people who dislike the theatre may include Molière in that dislike without ever having read a line of his or witnessed one of his plays; but nobody with any knowledge of Shakespear or Molière could possibly detest them, or read without pity and horror a description of their being insulted, tortured, and killed. And the same is true of Jesus. But it requires the most strenuous effort of conscience to refrain from crying "Serve him right" when we read of the stoning of Stephen; and nobody has ever cared twopence about the martyrdom of Peter: many better men have died worse deaths: for example, honest Hugh Latimer, who was burned by us, was worth fifty Stephens and a dozen Peters. One feels at last that when Jesus called Peter from his boat, he spoiled an honest fisherman, and made nothing better out of the wreck than a salvation monger.

The Controversies on Baptism and Transubstantiation

Meanwhile the inevitable effect of dropping the peculiar doctrines of Jesus and going back to John the Baptist, was to make it much easier to convert Gentiles than Jews; and it was by following the line of least resistance that Paul became the apostle to the Gentiles. The Jews had their own rite of initiation: the rite of circumcision; and they were fiercely jealous for it, because it marked them as the chosen people of God, and set them apart from the Gentiles, who were simply the uncircumcized. When Paul, finding that baptism made way faster among the Gentiles than among the Jews, as it enabled them to plead that they too were sanctified by a rite of later and higher authority than the Mosaic rite, he was compelled to admit that circumcision did not matter; and this, to the Jews, was an intolerable blasphemy. To

Gentiles like ourselves, a good deal of the Epistle to the Romans is now tedious to unreadableness because it consists of a hopeless attempt by Paul to evade the conclusion that if a man were baptized it did not matter a rap whether he was circumcized or not. Paul claims circumcision as an excellent thing in its way for a Jew; but if it has no efficacy towards salvation, and if salvation is the one thing needful—and Paul was committed to both propositions—his pleas in mitigation only made the Jews more determined to stone him.

Thus from the very beginning of apostolic Christianity, it was hampered by a dispute as to whether salvation was to be attained by a surgical operation or by a sprinkling of water: mere rites on which Jesus would not have wasted twenty words. Later on, when the new sect conquered the Gentile west, where the dispute had no practical application, the other ceremony—that of eating the god—produced a still more disastrous dispute, in which a difference of belief, not as to the obligation to perform the ceremony, but as to whether it was a symbolic or a real ingestion of divine substance, produced persecution, slaughter, hatred, and everything that Jesus loathed, on a monstrous scale.

But long before that, the superstitions which had fastened on the new faith made trouble. The parthenogenetic birth of Christ, simple enough at first as a popular miracle, was not left so simple by the theologians. They began to ask of what substance Christ was made in the womb of the virgin. When the Trinity was added to the faith the question arose, was the virgin the mother of God or only the mother of Jesus? Arian schisms and Nestorian schisms arose on these questions; and the leaders of the resultant agitations rancorously deposed one another and excommunicated one another according to their luck in enlisting the emperors on their side. In the IV century they began to burn one another for differences of opinion in such matters. In the VIII century Charlemagne made Christianity compulsory by killing those who refused to embrace it; and though this made an end of the voluntary character of conversion, Charlemagne may claim to be the first

Christian who put men to death for any point of doctrine that really mattered. From his time onward the history of Christian controversy reeks with blood and fire, torture and warfare. The Crusades, the persecutions in Albi and elsewhere, the Inquisition, the "wars of religion" which followed the Reformation, all presented themselves as Christian phenomena; but who can doubt that they would have been repudiated with horror by Jesus? Our own notion that the massacre of St Bartholomew's was an outrage on Christianity, whilst the campaigns of Gustavus Adolphus, and even of Frederick the Great, were a defence of it, is as absurd as the opposite notion that Frederick was Antichrist, and Torquemada and Ignatius Loyola men after the very heart of Jesus. Neither they nor their exploits had anything to do with him. It is probable that Archbishop Laud and John Wesley died equally persuaded that he in whose name they had made themselves famous on earth would receive them in Heaven with open arms. George Fox the Quaker would have had ten times their chance; and yet Fox made rather a miserable business of life.

Nevertheless all these perversions of the doctrine of Jesus derived their moral force from his credit, and so had to keep his gospel alive. When the Protestants translated the Bible into the vernacular and let it loose among the people, they did an extremely dangerous thing, as the mischief which followed proves; but they incidentally let loose the sayings of Jesus in open competition with the sayings of Paul and Koheleth and David and Solomon and the authors of Job and the Pentateuch; and, as we have seen, Jesus seems to be the winning name. The glaring contradiction between his teaching and the practice of all the States and all the Churches is no longer hidden. And it may be that though nineteen centuries have passed since Jesus was born (the date of his birth is now quaintly given as 7 B.C., though some contend for 100 B.C.), and though his Church has not yet been founded nor his political system tried, the bankruptcy of all the other systems when audited by our vital statistics, which give us a final test for all political systems, is driving us hard into accepting him, not as a scapegoat, but as one who was much less of a fool in practical matters than we have hitherto all thought him.

The Alternative Christs

Let us now clear up the situation a little. The New Testament tells two stories for two different sorts of readers. One is the old story of the achievement of our salvation by the sacrifice and atonement of a divine personage who was barbarously slain and rose again on the third day: the story as it was accepted by the apostles. And in this story the political, economic, and moral views of the Christ have no importance: the atonement is everything; and we are saved by our faith in it, and not by works or opinions (other than that particular opinion) bearing on practical affairs.

The other is the story of a prophet who, after expressing several very interesting opinions as to practical conduct, both personal and political, which are now of pressing importance, and instructing his disciples to carry them out in their daily life, lost his head; believed himself to be a crude legendary form of god; and under that delusion courted and suffered a cruel execution in the belief that he would rise from the dead and come in glory to reign over a regenerated world. In this form, the political, economic, and moral opinions of Jesus, as guides to conduct, are interesting and important: the rest is mere psychopathy and superstition. The accounts of the resurrection, the partheno-genetic birth, and the more incredible miracles are rejected as inventions; and such episodes as the conversation with the devil are classed with similar conversations recorded of St Dunstan, Luther, Bunyan, Swedenborg, and Blake.

Credulity no Criterion

This arbitrary acceptance and rejection of parts of the gospel is not peculiar to the Secularist view. We have seen Luke and

87

ANDROCLES AND THE LION

John reject Matthew's story of the massacre of the innocents and
the flight into Egypt without ceremony. The notion that Matthew's
manuscript is a literal and infallible record of facts, not subject to
the errors that beset all earthly chroniclers, would have made
John stare, being as it is a comparatively modern fancy of intellectually untrained people who keep the Bible on the same shelf
with Napoleon's Book of Fate, Old Moore's Almanack, and hand-
books of therapeutic herbalism. You may be a fanatical Salvationist and reject more miracle stories than Huxley did; and you
may utterly repudiate Jesus as the Savior and yet cite him as a
historical witness to the possession by men of the most marvellous
thaumaturgical powers. "Christ Scientist" and Jesus the Mahatma
are preached by people whom Peter would have struck dead as
worse infidels than Simon Magus; and the Atonement is preached
by Baptist and Congregationalist ministers whose views of the
miracles are those of Ingersoll and Bradlaugh. Luther, who made
a clean sweep of all the saints with their million miracles, and
reduced the Blessed Virgin herself to the status of an idol, con-
centrated Salvationism to a point at which the most execrable
murderer who believes in it when the rope is round his neck,
flies straight to the arms of Jesus, whilst Tom Paine and Shelley
fall into the bottomless pit to burn there to all eternity. And sceptical physicists like Sir William Crookes demonstrate by laboratory experiments that "mediums" like Dunglas Home can make
the pointer of a spring-balance go round without touching the
weight suspended from it.

BELIEF IN PERSONAL IMMORTALITY NO CRITERION

Nor is belief in individual immortality any criterion. Theosophists, rejecting vicarious atonement so sternly that they insist
that the smallest of our sins brings its Karma, also insist on individual immortality and metempyschosis in order to provide an
unlimited field for Karma to be worked out by the unredeemed
sinner. The belief in the prolongation of individual life beyond

the grave is far more real and vivid among table-rapping Spiritualists than among conventional Christians. The notion that those who reject the Christian (or any other) scheme of salvation by atonement must reject also belief in personal immortality and in miracles is as baseless as the notion that if a man is an atheist he will steal your watch.

I could multiply these instances to weariness. The main difference that set Gladstone and Huxley by the ears is not one between belief in supernatural persons or miraculous events and the sternest view of such belief as a breach of intellectual integrity: it is the difference between belief in the efficacy of the crucifixion as an infallible cure for guilt, and a congenital incapacity for believing this, or (the same thing) desiring to believe it.

The Secular View Natural, not Rational, therefore Inevitable

It must therefore be taken as a flat fundamental modern fact, whether we like it or not, that whilst many of us cannot believe that Jesus got his curious grip of our souls by mere sentimentality, neither can we believe that he was John Barleycorn. The more our reason and study lead us to believe that Jesus was talking the most penetrating good sense when he preached Communism; when he declared that the reality behind the popular belief in God was a creative spirit in ourselves called by him the Heavenly Father and by us Evolution, Élan Vital, Life Force and other names; when he protested against the claims of marriage and the family to appropriate that high part of our energy that was meant for the service of his Father, the more impossible it becomes for us to believe that he was talking equally good sense when he so suddenly announced that he was himself a visible concrete God; that his flesh and blood were miraculous food for us; that he must be tortured and slain in the traditional manner and would rise from the dead after three days; and that at his Second Coming the stars would fall from heaven and he become king of an earthly paradise. But it is easy and reasonable to believe that an over-wrought preacher at last went mad as Swift and Ruskin and Nietzsche went mad. Every asylum has in it a patient suffering from the delusion that he is a god, yet otherwise sane enough. These patients do not nowadays declare that they will be barbar-ously slain and will rise from the dead, because they have lost that tradition of the destiny of godhead; but they claim every-thing appertaining to divinity that is within their knowledge.

Thus the gospels as memoirs and suggestive statements of sociological and biological doctrine, highly relevant to modern civilization, though ending in the history of a psychopathic de-lusion, are quite credible, intelligible, and interesting to modern thinkers. In any other light they are neither credible, intelligible, nor interesting except to people upon whom the delusion imposes.

"THE HIGHER CRITICISM"

Historical research and paleographic criticism will no doubt continue their demonstrations that the New Testament, like the Old, seldom tells a single story or expounds a single doctrine, and gives us often an accretion and conglomeration of widely discrete and even unrelated traditions and doctrines. But these disintegra-tions, though technically interesting to scholars, and gratifying or exasperating, as the case may be, to people who are merely defending or attacking the paper fortifications of the infallibility of the Bible, have hardly anything to do with the purpose of these pages. I have mentioned the fact that most of the authorities are now agreed (for the moment) that the date of the birth of Jesus may be placed at about 7 B.C.; but they do not therefore date their letters 1923, nor, I presume, do they expect me to do so. What I am engaged in is a criticism (in the Kantian sense) of an established body of belief which has become an actual part of the mental fabric of my readers; and I should be the most exasperat-ing of triflers and pedants if I were to digress into a criticism of some other belief or nobelief which my readers might conceivably profess if they were erudite Scriptural paleographers and historians, in which case, by the way, they would have to change their views so frequently that the gospel they received in their childhood would dominate them after all by its superior persistency. The chaos of mere facts in which the Sermon on the Mount and the Ode to Charity suggest nothing but disputes as to whether they are interpolations or not, in which Jesus becomes nothing but a name suspected of belonging to ten different prophets or executed persons, in which Paul is only the man who could not possibly have written the epistles attributed to him, in which Chinese sages, Greek philosophers, Latin authors, and writers of ancient anonymous inscriptions are thrown at our heads as the sources of this or that scrap of the Bible, is neither a religion nor a criticism of religion: one does not offer the fact that a good deal of the medieval building in Peterborough Cathedral was found to be flagrant jerry-building as a criticism of the Dean's sermons. For good or evil, we have made a synthesis out of the literature we call the Bible; and though the discovery that there is a good deal of jerry-building in the Bible is interesting in its way, because everything about the Bible is interesting, it does not alter the synthesis very materially even for the paleographers, and does not alter it at all for those who know no more about modern paleography than Archbishop Ussher did. I have therefore indicated little more of the discoveries than Archbishop Ussher might have guessed for himself if he had read the Bible without prepossessions.

For the rest, I have taken the synthesis as it really lives and works in men. After all, a synthesis is what you want: it is the case you have to judge brought to an apprehensible issue for you. Even if you have little more respect for synthetic biography than for synthetic rubber, synthetic milk, and the still unachieved synthetic protoplasm which is to enable us to make different sorts of men as a pastrycook makes different sorts of tarts, the practical issue still lies as plainly before you as before the most credulous votaries of what pontificates as the Higher Criticism.

G

The Perils of Salvationism

The secular view of Jesus is powerfully reinforced by the increase in our day of the number of people who have had the means of educating and training themselves to the point at which they are not afraid to look facts in the face, even such terrifying facts as sin and death. The result is greater sternness in modern thought. The conviction is spreading that to encourage a man to believe that though his sins be as scarlet he can be made whiter than snow by an easy exercise of self-conceit, is to encourage him to be a rascal. It did not work so badly when you could also conscientiously assure him that if he let himself be caught napping in the matter of faith by death, a red-hot hell would roast him alive to all eternity. In those days a sudden death—the most enviable of all deaths—was regarded as the most frightful calamity. It was classed with plague, pestilence, and famine, battle and murder, in our prayers. But belief in that hell is fast vanishing. All the leaders of thought have lost it; and even for the rank and file it has fled to those parts of Ireland and Scotland which are still in the seventeenth century. Even there, it is tacitly reserved for the other fellow.

The Importance of Hell in the Salvation Scheme

The seriousness of throwing over hell whilst still clinging to the Atonement is obvious. If there is no punishment for sin there can be no self-forgiveness for it. If Christ paid our score, and if there is no hell and therefore no chance of our getting into trouble by forgetting the obligation, then we can be as wicked as we like with impunity inside the secular law, even from self-reproach, which becomes mere ingratitude to the Savior. On the other hand, if Christ did not pay our score, it still stands against us; and such debts make us extremely uncomfortable. The drive of evolution, which we call conscience and honor, seizes on such slips, and shames us to the dust for being so low in the scale as to be capable of them. The "saved" thief experiences an ecstatic happiness which can never come to the honest atheist: he is tempted to steal again to repeat the glorious sensation. But if the atheist steals he has no such happiness. He is a thief and knows that he is a thief. Nothing can rub that off him. He may try to soothe his shame by some sort of restitution or equivalent act of benevolence; but that does not alter the fact that he did steal; and his conscience will not be easy until he has conquered his will to steal and changed himself into an honest man by developing that divine spark within him which Jesus insisted on as the everyday reality of what the atheist denies.

Now though the state of the believers in the Atonement may thus be the happier, it is most certainly not more desirable from the point of view of the community. The fact that a believer is happier than a sceptic is no more to the point than the fact that a drunken man is happier than a sober one. The happiness of credulity is a cheap and dangerous quality of happiness, and by no means a necessity of life. Whether Socrates got as much happiness out of life as Wesley is an unanswerable question; but a nation of Socrateses would be much safer and happier than a nation of Wesleys; and its individuals would be higher in the evolutionary scale. At all events it is in the Socratic man and not in the Wesleyan that our hope lies now.

THE RIGHT TO REFUSE ATONEMENT

Consequently, even if it were mentally possible for all of us to believe in the Atonement, we should have to cry off it, as we evidently have a right to do. Every man to whom salvation is offered has an inalienable natural right to say "No, thank you: I prefer to retain my full moral responsibility: it is not good for me to be able to load a scapegoat with my sins: I should be less careful how I committed them if I knew they would cost me nothing." Then, too, there is the attitude of Ibsen: that iron moralist to whom the whole scheme of salvation was only an ignoble attempt to cheat God; to get into heaven without paying the price. To be let off, to beg for and accept eternal life as a present instead of earning it, would be mean enough even if we accepted the contempt of the Power on whose pity we were trading; but to bargain for a crown of glory as well! that was too much for Ibsen: it provoked him to exclaim, "Your God is an old man whom you cheat," and to lash the deadened conscience of the nineteenth century back to life with a whip of scorpions.

THE TEACHING OF CHRISTIANITY

And there I must leave the matter to such choice as your nature allows you. The honest teacher who has to make known to a novice the facts about Christianity cannot in any essential regard, I think, put the facts otherwise than as I have put them. If children are to be delivered from the proselytizing atheist on the one hand, and the proselytizing nun in the convent school on the other, with all the other proselytizers that lie between them, they must not be burdened with idle controversies as to whether there was ever such a person as Jesus or not. When Hume said that Joshua's campaigns were impossible, Whately did not wrangle about it: he proved, on the same lines, that the campaigns of Napoleon were impossible. Only fictitious characters will stand Hume's sort of examination: nothing will ever make Edward the Confessor and St Louis as real to us as Don Quixote and Mr Pickwick. We must cut the controversy short by declaring that there is the same evidence for the existence of Jesus as for that of any other person of his time; and the fact that you may not believe everything Matthew tells you no more disproves the existence of Jesus than the fact that you do not believe everything Macaulay tells you disproves the existence of William III. The gospel narratives in the main give you a biography which is quite credible and accountable on purely secular grounds when you have trimmed off everything that Hume or Grimm or Rousseau or Huxley or any modern bishop could reject as fanciful. Without going further than this, you can become a follower of Jesus just as you can become a follower of Confucius or Lao Tse, and may therefore call yourself a Jesuist, or even a Christian, if you hold, as the strictest Secularist quite legitimately may, that all prophets are inspired, and all men with a mission, Christs.

The teacher of Christianity has then to make known to the child, first the song of John Barleycorn, with the fields and seasons as witness to its eternal truth. Then, as the child's mind matures, it can learn, as historical and psychological phenomena, the tradition of the scapegoat, the Redeemer, the Atonement, the Resurrection, the Second Coming, and how, in a world saturated with this tradition, Jesus has been largely accepted as the long expected and often prophesied Redeemer, the Messiah, *the* Christ. It is open to the child also to accept him. If the child is built like Gladstone, he will accept Jesus as his Savior, and Peter and John the Baptist as the Savior's revealer and forerunner respectively. If he is built like Huxley, he will take the secular view, in spite of all that a pious family can do to prevent him. The important thing now is that the Gladstones and Huxleys should no longer waste their time irrelevantly and ridiculously wrangling about the Gadarene swine, and that they should make up their minds as to the soundness of the secular doctrines of Jesus; for it is about these that they may come to blows in our own time.

CHRISTIANITY AND THE EMPIRE

Finally, let us ask why it is that the old superstitions have so suddenly lost countenance that although, to the utter disgrace of the nation's leaders and rulers, the laws by which persecutors can destroy or gag all freedom of thought and speech in these matters are still unrepealed and ready to the hand of our bigots and fanatics (quite recently a respectable shopkeeper was convicted of "blasphemy" for saying that if a modern girl accounted for an illicit pregnancy by saying she had conceived of the Holy Ghost, we should know what to think: a remark which would never have occurred to him had he been properly taught how the story was grafted on the gospel), yet somehow they are used only against poor men, and that only in a half-hearted way. When we consider that from the time when the first scholar ventured to whisper as a professional secret that the Pentateuch could not possibly have been written by Moses to the time within my own recollection when Bishop Colenso, for saying the same thing openly, was inhibited from preaching and actually excommunicated, eight centuries elapsed (the point at issue, though technically interesting to paleographers and historians, having no more bearing on human welfare than the controversy as to whether uncial or cursive is the older form of writing); yet now, within fifty years of Colenso's heresy, there is not a Churchman of any authority living, or an educated layman, who could without ridicule declare that Moses wrote the Pentateuch as Pascal wrote his Thoughts or D'Aubigny his History of the Reformation, or that St Jerome wrote the passage about the three witnesses in the Vulgate, or that there are less than three different accounts of the creation jumbled together in the book of Genesis. Now the maddest Progressive will hardly contend that our growth in wisdom and liberality has been greater in the last half century than in the sixteen half centuries preceding: indeed it would be easier to sustain the thesis that the last fifty years have witnessed a distinct reaction from Victorian Liberalism to Collectivism which has perceptibly strengthened the State Churches. Yet the fact remains that whereas Byron's Cain, published a century ago, is a leading case on the point that there is no copyright in a blasphemous book, the Salvation Army might now include it among its publications without shocking anyone.

I suggest that the causes which have produced this sudden clearing of the air include the transformation of many modern States, notably the old self-contained French Republic and the tight little Island of Britain, into empires which overflow the frontiers of all the Churches. In India, for example, there are less than four million Christians out of a population of three hundred and sixteen and a half millions. The King of England is the defender of the faith; but what faith is now *the* faith? The inhabitants of this island would, within the memory of persons still living, have claimed that their faith is surely *the* faith of God, and that all others are heathen. But we islanders are only forty-five millions; and if we count ourselves all as Christians, there are still seventy-seven and a quarter million Mahometans in the Empire. Add to these the Hindoos and Buddhists, Sikhs and Jains, whom I was taught in my childhood, by way of religious instruction, to regard as gross idolaters consigned to eternal perdition, but whose faith I can now be punished for disparaging by a provocative word, and you have a total of over three hundred and forty-two and a quarter million heretics to swamp our forty-five million Britons, of whom, by the way, only six thousand call themselves distinctively "disciples of Christ," the rest being members of the Church of England and other denominations whose discipleship is less emphatically affirmed. In short, the Englishman of today, instead of being, like the forefathers whose ideas he clings to, a subject of a State practically wholly Christian, is now crowded, and indeed considerably overcrowded, into a corner of an Empire in which the Christians are a mere eleven per cent of the population; so that the Nonconformist who allows his umbrella stand to be sold up rather than pay rates towards the support of a Church of England school, finds himself paying taxes not only to endow the Church of Rome in Malta, but to send Christians to prison for the blasphemy of offering Bibles for sale in the streets of Khartoum.

Turn to France, a country ten times more insular in its preoccupation with its own language, its own history, its own character, than we, who have always been explorers and colonizers and grumblers. This once self-centred nation is forty millions strong. The total population of the French Republic is about one hundred and fourteen millions. The French are not in our hopeless Christian minority of eleven per cent; but they are in a minority of thirty-five per cent, which is fairly conclusive. And, being a more logical people than we, they have officially abandoned Christianity and declared that the French State has no specific religion.

Neither has the British State, though it does not say so. No doubt there are many innocent people in England who take Charlemagne's view, and would, as a matter of course, offer our eighty-nine per cent of "pagans, I regret to say" the alternative of death or Christianity but for a vague impression that these lost ones are all being converted gradually by the missionaries. But no statesman can entertain such ludicrously parochial delusions. No English king or French president can possibly govern on the assumption that the theology of Peter and Paul, Luther and Calvin, has any objective validity, or that the Christ is more than the Buddha, or Jehovah more than Krishna, or Jesus more or less human than Mahomet or Zoroaster or Confucius. He is actually compelled, in so far as he makes laws against blasphemy at all, to treat all the religions, including Christianity, as blasphemous when paraded before people who are not accustomed to them and do not want them. And even that is a concession to a mischievous intolerance which an empire should use its control of education to eradicate.

On the other hand, Governments cannot really divest themselves of religion, or even of dogma. When Jesus said that people should not only live but live more abundantly, he was dogmatizing; and many Pessimist sages, including Shakespear, whose hero begged his friend to refrain from suicide in the words "Absent thee from felicity awhile," would say dogmatizing very perniciously. Indeed many preachers and saints declare, some of them in the name of Jesus himself, that this world is a vale of tears, and that our lives had better be passed in sorrow and even in torment, as a preparation for a better life to come. Make these sad people comfortable; and they baffle you by putting on hair shirts.

None the less, Governments must proceed on dogmatic assumptions, whether they call them dogmas or not; and they must clearly be assumptions common enough to stamp those who reject them as eccentrics or lunatics. And the greater and more heterogeneous the population the commoner the assumptions must be. A Trappist monastery can be conducted on assumptions which would in twenty-four hours provoke the village at its gates to insurrection. That is because the monastery selects its people; and if a Trappist does not like it he can leave it. But a subject of the British Empire or the French Republic is not selected; and if he does not like it he must lump it; for emigration is practicable only within narrow limits, and seldom provides an effective remedy, all civilizations being now much alike.

To anyone capable of comprehending government at all it must be evident without argument that the set of fundamental assumptions drawn up in the thirty-nine articles or in the Westminster Confession are wildly impossible as political constitutions for modern empires. A personal profession of them by any person disposed to take such professions seriously would practically disqualify him for high imperial office. A Calvinist Viceroy of India and a Particular Baptist Secretary of State for Foreign Affairs would wreck the empire. The Stuarts wrecked even the tight little island which was the nucleus of the empire by their Scottish logic and theological dogma; and it may be sustained very plausibly that the alleged aptitude of the English for self-government, which is contradicted by every chapter of their history, is really only an incurable inaptitude for theology, and indeed for co-ordinated thought in any direction, which makes them equally impatient of systematic despotism and systematic good government: their history being that of a badly governed and accidentally free people (comparatively). Thus our success in colonizing, as far as it has not been produced by exterminating the natives, has been due to our indifference to the salvation of our subjects. Ireland is the exception which proves the rule; for Ireland, the standing instance of the inability of the English to colonize without extermination of natives, is also the one country under British rule in which the conquerors and colonizers proceeded on the assumption that their business was to establish

Protestantism as well as to make money and thereby secure at least the lives of the unfortunate inhabitants out of whose labor it could be made. At this moment Ulster is refusing to accept fellow-citizenship with the other Irish provinces because the south believes in St Peter and Bossuet, and the north in St Paul and Calvin. Imagine the effect of trying to govern India or Egypt from Belfast or from the Vatican!

The position is perhaps graver for France than for England, because the sixty-five per cent of French subjects who are neither French nor Christian nor Modernist includes some thirty millions of negroes who are susceptible, and indeed highly susceptible, of conversion to those salvationist forms of pseudo-Christianity which have produced all the persecutions and religious wars of the last fifteen hundred years. When the late explorer Sir Henry Stanley told me of the emotional grip which Christianity had over the Baganda tribes, and read me their letters, which were exactly like medieval letters in their literal faith and ever-present piety, I said "Can these men handle a rifle?" To which Stanley replied with some scorn "Of course they can, as well as any white man." Now at this moment (1915) a vast European war is being waged, in which the French are using Senegalese soldiers. I ask the French Government, which, like our own Government, is deliberately leaving the religious instruction of these negroes in the hands of missions of Petrine Catholics and Pauline Calvinists, whether they have considered the possibility of a new series of crusades, by ardent African Salvationists, to rescue Paris from the grip of the modern scientific "infidel," and to raise the cry of "Back to the Apostles: back to Charlemagne!"

We are more fortunate in that an overwhelming majority of our subjects are Hindoos, Mahometans, and Buddhists; that is, they have, as a prophylactic against salvationist Christianity, highly civilized religions of their own. Mahometanism, which Napoleon at the end of his career classed as perhaps the best popular religion for modern political use, might in some respects have arisen as a reformed Christianity if Mahomet had had to deal with a population of seventeenth-century Christians instead of Arabs who worshipped stones. As it is, men do not reject Mahomet for Calvin; and to offer a Hindoo so crude a theology as ours in exchange for his own, or our Jewish canonical literature as an improvement on Hindoo scripture, is to offer old lamps for older ones in a market where the oldest lamps, like old furniture in England, are the most highly valued.

Yet, I repeat, government is impossible without a religion: that is, without a body of common assumptions. The open mind never acts: when we have done our utmost to arrive at a reasonable conclusion, we still, when we can reason and investigate no more, must close our minds for the moment with a snap, and act dogmatically on our conclusions. The man who waits to make an entirely reasonable will dies intestate. A man so reasonable as to have an open mind about theft and murder, or about the need for food and reproduction, might just as well be a fool and a scoundrel for any use he could be as a legislator or a State official. The modern pseudo-democratic statesman, who says that he is only in power to carry out the will of the people, and moves only as the cat jumps, is clearly a political and intellectual brigand. The rule of the negative man who has no convictions means in practice the rule of the positive mob. Freedom of conscience as Cromwell used the phrase is an excellent thing; nevertheless if any man had proposed to give effect to freedom of conscience as to cannibalism in England, Cromwell would have laid him by the heels almost as promptly as he would have laid a Roman Catholic, though in Fiji at the same moment he would have supported heartily the freedom of conscience of a vegetarian who disparaged the sacred diet of Long Pig.

Here then comes in the importance of the repudiation by Jesus of proselytism. His rule "Dont pull up the tares: sow the wheat: if you try to pull up the tares you will pull up the wheat with it" is the only possible rule for a statesman governing a modern empire, or a voter supporting such a statesman. There is nothing in the teaching of Jesus that cannot be assented to by a Brahman, a

Mahometan, a Buddhist or a Jew, without any question of their conversion to Christianity. In some ways it is easier to reconcile a Mahometan to Jesus than a British parson, because the idea of a professional priest is unfamiliar and even monstrous to a Mahometan (the tourist who persists in asking who is the dean of St Sophia puzzles beyond words the sacristan who lends him a huge pair of slippers); and Jesus never suggested that his disciples should separate themselves from the laity: he picked them up by the wayside, where any man or woman might follow him. For priests he had not a civil word; and they shewed their sense of his hostility by getting him killed as soon as possible. He was, in short, a thorough-going anti-Clerical. And though, as we have seen, it is only by political means that his doctrine can be put into practice, he not only never suggested a sectarian theocracy as a form of government, and would certainly have prophesied the downfall of the late President Kruger if he had survived to his time, but, when challenged, he refused to teach his disciples not to pay tribute to Caesar, admitting that Caesar, who presumably had the kingdom of heaven within him as much as any disciple, had his place in the scheme of things. Indeed the apostles made this an excuse for carrying subservience to the State to a pitch of idolatry that ended in the theory of the divine right of kings, and provoked men to cut kings' heads off to restore some sense of proportion in the matter. Jesus certainly did not consider the overthrow of the Roman empire or the substitution of a new ecclesiastical organization for the Jewish Church or for the priesthood of the Roman gods as part of his program. He said that God was better than Mammon; but he never said that Tweedledum was better than Tweedledee; and that is why it is now possible for British citizens and statesmen to follow Jesus, though they cannot possibly follow either Tweedledum or Tweedledee without bringing the empire down with a crash on their heads. And at that I must leave it.

LONDON, *December* 1915

Prefatory Note

(From the programme of the St James's Theatre,
London, 1 September 1913)

The version of the old story of Androcles and the Lion to be
played to-night at the St James's Theatre is not hampered by a
pedantic retention of the details as given by Aulus Gellius. His
Androcles was called Androclus, and Androclus was neither a
Greek nor a tailor nor a Christian, but a Roman slave who ran
away from the cruelties of his master and was later on captured
and condemned to be devoured by wild beasts in the arena. But
it happened that during his flight he had taken refuge in a cave;
and into this cave came a lion who had a thorn in his paw which
Androclus extracted. It was to this very lion that Androclus was
afterwards thrown in the arena; and the lion, instead of eating
him, caressed him. The story figured in natural histories like
those of Aelian and was found to please children, in whose story
books it has appeared ever since. Nobody believes it; though
everybody believes much more improbable stories. It would be
incredible of some lions just as the action of Androclus would be
incredible of some men. But there are lions and lions, just as
there are men and men. The author of the present version has
petted a full-grown lion and had his advances received with
much more cordiality than he·could expect from most St
Bernard dogs. He conceives the lion of Androclus to have been
just such a fearless and amiable creature. He conceives Androclus as having that fellow feeling for animals which it becomes
the most highly evolved of animals to have (Man is your real
king of beasts) and which enables some men to handle bees
without being stung and snakes without being bitten. Given
such a pair, there is nothing incredible in the story except the
theatrical coincidence of the meeting of the two in the arena.
Such coincidences are privileged on the stage, and are the
special delight of this particular author. And really, when one

considers how many men met lions in the arena from first to last, it is not too much to ask you to believe that just for once they turned out to be old friends.

If the author is asked why he has made Androcles a Christian, he can only ask why not. St Francis preached to the birds as to his "little brothers"; and St Francis was a Christian. St Anthony preached to the fishes, who probably understood at least as much of his sermon as a modern fashionable congregation would have done; and St Anthony was a Christian. Depend on it, Androcles had that root of the religious matter in him which made all religions free to him except the religion of hunting and killing. That is, the religion of the English country house.

But the twentieth-century Christian need not regard the Christianity of the early Christian martyrs as having much to do with his safe and eminently respectable Sunday profession of faith. Christians in those days were neither safe nor respectable. What is more, some of the most eminent Christians were by no means fond of the average Christians of their time. The author once asked an old Owenite Socialist why he had given up Socialism. He replied that after preaching it for some years he had noticed that it seemed to have a very bad effect on the moral character of those who gave themselves up to its propaganda. The same may be said of all persecuted creeds. A doctrine may be true and important, and its persecutors may be altogether in the wrong; but this makes the position of the man who is persecuted for propagating it all the more morbid. One sane man in a lunatic asylum can no more keep his normal health and temper than one lunatic in a *conseil de prudhommes*. Add to this consideration the fact that all movements which attack the existing state of society attract both the people who are not good enough for the world and the people for whom the world is not good enough; so that the saint is always embarrassed by finding that the dynamiter and the assassin, the thief and the libertine, make common cause with him; and you will not be surprised to learn, if you do not know it already, that early Christians like

PREFATORY NOTE

Saint Augustine have a good many stories to tell of Christians who thoroughly deserved their evil reputation. The character of Spintho in the present play is by no means a malicious invention of the author's. Indeed had he gone on to exhibit Spintho as having taken the precaution to marry an orthodox Roman in order to shirk the Christian obligation to practise Communism, and as ostentatiously giving the lady black eyes to show how his conjugal duties revolted his ascetic nature, there would have been warrant for that too, and worse, in the records of the Fathers of the Church.

In representing a Roman centurion and a Roman captain (a pure invention) as corresponding to a British sergeant and a British company officer, some violence may or may not have been done to the petty accuracies of military history. Centurions were much chaffed in Rome as being mostly thick-booted vulgar persons, whacking their men with vinewood cudgels, and out of place in refined society; and the nearest thing to a modern captain as far as rank was concerned was probably not much more of a patrician. The patrician soldier was not a professional soldier: he commanded armies or adorned Senates or governed provinces as part of the natural pursuits of a patrician. But the relation of patrician officer to plebeian routineer existed as it exists to-day; and whether my captain should have been called something else, or my Centurion a Decurion, does not trouble me any more than the old controversy as to whether the audience turned their thumbs up or down when they wanted a defeated gladiator slain.

In short, if you demand my authorities for this and that, I must reply that only those who have never hunted up the authorities as I have believe that there is any authority who is not contradicted flatly by some other authority. Marshal Junot, reproached for having no respect for ancestry, said that he was an ancestor himself. In the same spirit I point out that the authorities on the story of Androcles and on the history of the early Christian martyrs are the people who have written about them; and now that I, too, have written about them, I take my place as the latest authority on the subject and ask you to respect me accordingly.

G. B. S.

Not to in tro. Meg —
But to show Androcl —'s
attitudes, mannerisms.

ANDROCLES AND THE LION

PROLOGUE

Overture: forest sounds, roaring of lions, Christian hymn faintly.

A jungle path. A lion's roar, a melancholy suffering roar, comes from the jungle. It is repeated nearer. The lion limps from the jungle on three legs, holding up his right forepaw, in which a huge thorn sticks. He sits down and contemplates it. He licks it. He shakes it. He tries to extract it by scraping it along the ground, and hurts himself worse. He roars piteously. He licks it again. Tears drop from his eyes. He limps painfully off the path and lies down under the trees, exhausted with pain. Heaving a long sigh, like wind in a trombone, he goes to sleep.

Androcles and his wife Megaera come along the path. He is a small, thin, ridiculous little man who might be any age from thirty to fifty-five. He has sandy hair, watery compassionate blue eyes, sensitive nostrils, and a very presentable forehead; but his good points go no further: his arms and legs and back, though wiry of their kind, look shrivelled and starved. He carries a big bundle, is very poorly clad, and seems tired and hungry.

His wife is a rather handsome pampered slattern, well fed and in the prime of life. She has nothing to carry, and has a stout stick to help her along.

MEGAERA [*suddenly throwing down her stick*] I wont go another step.

ANDROCLES [*pleading wearily*] Oh, not again, dear. Whats the good of stopping every two miles and saying you wont go another step? We must get on to the next village before night. There are wild beasts in this wood: lions, they say.

MEGAERA. I dont believe a word of it. You are always threatening me with wild beasts to make me walk the very soul out of my body when I can hardly drag one foot before another. We havnt seen a single lion yet.

107

ANDROCLES. Well, dear, do you want to see one?

MEGAERA [*tearing the bundle from his back*] You cruel brute, you dont care how tired I am, or what becomes of me [*she throws the bundle on the ground*]: always thinking of yourself. Self! self! self! always yourself! [*She sits down on the bundle*].

ANDROCLES [*sitting down sadly on the ground with his elbows on his knees and his head in his hands*] We all have to think of ourselves occasionally, dear.

MEGAERA. A man ought to think of his wife sometimes.

ANDROCLES. He cant always help it, dear. You make me think of you a good deal. Not that I blame you.

MEGAERA. Blame me! I should think not indeed. Is it my fault that I'm married to you?

ANDROCLES. No, dear: that is my fault.

MEGAERA. Thats a nice thing to say to me. Arnt you happy with me?

ANDROCLES. I dont complain, my love.

MEGAERA. You ought to be ashamed of yourself.

ANDROCLES. I am, my dear.

MEGAERA. Youre not: you glory in it.

ANDROCLES. In what, darling?

MEGAERA. In everything. In making me a slave, and making yourself a laughing-stock. It's not fair. You get me the name of being a shrew with your meek ways, always talking as if butter wouldnt melt in your mouth. And just because I look a big strong woman, and because I'm goodhearted and a bit hasty, and because youre always driving me to do things I'm sorry for afterwards, people say "Poor man: what a life his wife leads him!" Oh, if they only knew! And you think I dont know. But I do, I do, [*screaming*] I do.

ANDROCLES. Yes, my dear: I know you do.

MEGAERA. Then why dont you treat me properly and be a good husband to me?

ANDROCLES. What can I do, my dear?

MEGAERA. What can you do! You can return to your duty, and

come back to your home and your friends, and sacrifice to the gods as all respectable people do, instead of having us hunted out of house and home for being dirty disreputable blaspheming atheists.

ANDROCLES. I'm not an atheist, dear: I am a Christian.

MEGAERA. Well, isnt that the same thing, only ten times worse? Everybody knows that the Christians are the very lowest of the low.

ANDROCLES. Just like us, dear.

MEGAERA. Speak for yourself. Dont you dare to compare me to common people. My father owned his own public-house; and sorrowful was the day for me when you first came drinking in our bar.

ANDROCLES. I confess I was addicted to it, dear. But I gave it up when I became a Christian.

MEGAERA. Youd much better have remained a drunkard. I can forgive a man being addicted to drink: it's only natural; and I dont deny I like a drop myself sometimes. What I cant stand is your being addicted to Christianity. And whats worse again, your being addicted to animals. How is any woman to keep her house clean when you bring in every stray cat and lost cur and lame duck in the whole countryside ? You took the bread out of my mouth to feed them: you know you did: dont attempt to deny it.

ANDROCLES. Only when they were hungry and you were getting too stout, dearie.

MEGAERA. Yes: insult me, do. [*Rising*] Oh! I wont bear it another moment. You used to sit and talk to those dumb brute beasts for hours, when you hadnt a word for me.

ANDROCLES. They never answered back, darling. [*He rises and again shoulders the bundle*].

MEGAERA. Well, if youre fonder of animals than of your own wife, you can live with them here in the jungle. Ive had enough of them and enough of you. I'm going back. I'm going home.

ANDROCLES [*barring the way back*] No, dearie: dont take on

like that. We cant go back. Weve sold everything: we should starve; and I should be sent to Rome and thrown to the lions—

MEGAERA. Serve you right! I wish the lions joy of you. [*Screaming*] Are you going to get out of my way and let me go home?

ANDROCLES. No, dear—

MEGAERA. Then I'll make my way through the forest; and when I'm eaten by the wild beasts youll know what a wife youve lost. [*She dashes into the jungle and nearly falls over the sleeping lion*]. Oh! Oh! Andy! Andy! [*She totters back and collapses into the arms of Androcles, who, crushed by her weight, falls on his bundle*].

ANDROCLES [*extracting himself from beneath her and slapping her hands in great anxiety*] What is it, my precious, my pet? Whats the matter? [*He raises her head. Speechless with terror, she points in the direction of the sleeping lion. He steals cautiously towards the spot indicated by Megaera. She rises with an effort and totters after him*].

MEGAERA. No, Andy: youll be killed. Come back.

The lion utters a long snoring sigh. Androcles sees the lion, and recoils fainting into the arms of Megaera, who falls back on the bundle. They roll apart and lie staring in terror at one another. The lion is heard groaning heavily in the jungle.

ANDROCLES [*whispering*] Did you see? A lion.

MEGAERA [*despairing*] The gods have sent him to punish us because youre a Christian. Take me away, Andy. Save me.

ANDROCLES [*rising*] Meggy: theres one chance for you. Itll take him pretty nigh twenty minutes to eat me (I'm rather stringy and tough) and you can escape in less time than that.

MEGAERA. Oh, dont talk about eating. [*The lion rises with a great groan and limps towards them*]. Oh! [*She faints*].

ANDROCLES [*quaking, but keeping between the lion and Megaera*] Dont you come near my wife, do you hear? [*The lion groans. Androcles can hardly stand for trembling*]. Meggy: run. Run for your life. If I take my eye off him, it's all up. [*The lion holds up his wounded paw and flaps it piteously before Androcles*]. Oh, he's lame, poor old chap! He's got a thorn in his paw. A frightfully big thorn. [*Full of sympathy*] Oh, poor old man! Did um get an awful thorn into um's tootsums wootsums? Has it made um too sick to eat a nice little Christian man for um's breakfast? Oh, a nice little Christian man will get um's thorn out for um; and then um shall eat the nice Christian man and the nice Christian man's nice big tender wifey pifey. [*The lion responds by moans of self-pity*]. Yes, yes, yes, yes, yes. Now, now [*taking the paw in his hand*], um is not to bite and not to scratch, not even if it hurts a very very little. Now make velvet paws. Thats right. [*He pulls gingerly at the thorn. The lion, with an angry yell of pain, jerks back his paw so abruptly that Androcles is thrown on his back*]. Steadeee! Oh, did the nasty cruel little Christian man hurt the sore paw? [*The lion moans assentingly but apologetically*]. Well, one more little pull and it will be all over. Just one little, little, leetle pull; and then um will live happily ever after. [*He gives the thorn another pull. The lion roars and snaps his jaws with a terrifying clash*]. Oh, mustnt frighten um's good kind doctor, um's affectionate nursey. That didnt hurt at all: not a bit. Just one more. Just to shew how the brave big lion can bear pain, not like the little crybaby Christian man. Oopsh! [*The thorn comes out. The lion yells with pain, and shakes his paw wildly*]. Thats it! [*Holding up the thorn*]. Now it's out. Now lick um's paw to take away the nasty inflammation. See? [*He licks his own hand. The lion nods intelligently and licks his paw industriously*]. Clever little liony-piony! Understands um's dear old friend Andy Wandy. [*The lion licks his face*]. Yes, kissums Andy Wandy. [*The lion wagging his tail violently, rises on his hind legs, and embraces Androcles, who makes a wry face and cries*] Velvet paws! Velvet paws! [*The lion draws in his claws*]. Thats right. [*He embraces the lion, who finally takes the end of his tail in one paw, places that tight round Androcles' waist, resting it on his hip. Androcles takes the other paw in his hand, stretches out his arm, and the two waltz rapturously round and round and finally away through the jungle*].

H

MEGAERA [*who has revived during the waltz*] Oh, you coward, you havnt danced with me for years; and now you go off dancing with a great brute beast that you havnt known for ten minutes and that wants to eat your own wife. Coward. Coward! Coward! [*She rushes off after them into the jungle*].

ACT I

Evening. The end of three converging roads to Rome. Three triumphal arches span them where they debouch on a square at the gate of the city. Looking north through the arches one can see the campagna threaded by the three long dusty tracks. On the east and west sides of the square are long stone benches. An old beggar sits on the east side, his bowl at his feet.

Through the eastern arch a squad of Roman soldiers tramps along escorting a batch of Christian prisoners of both sexes and all ages, among them one Lavinia, a good-looking resolute young woman, apparently of higher social standing than her fellow prisoners. A centurion, carrying his vinewood cudgel, trudges alongside the squad, on its right, in command of it. All are tired and dusty; but the soldiers are dogged and indifferent, the Christians lighthearted and determined to treat their hardships as a joke and encourage one another.

A bugle is heard far behind on the road, where the rest of the cohort is following.

CENTURION [*stopping*] Halt! Orders from the Captain. [*They halt and wait*]. Now then, you Christians, none of your larks. The captain's coming. Mind you behave yourselves. No singing. Look respectful. Look serious, if youre capable of it. See that big building over there! Thats the Coliseum. Thats where youll be thrown to the lions or set to fight the gladiators presently. Think of that; and itll help you to behave properly before the captain. [*The Captain arrives*]. Attention! Salute! [*The soldiers salute*].

A CHRISTIAN [*cheerfully*] God bless you, Captain!

THE CENTURION [*scandalized*] Silence!

The Captain, a patrician, handsome, about thirty-five, very cold and distinguished, very superior and authoritative, steps up on a stone seat at the west side of the square, behind the centurion, so as to dominate the others more effectually.

113

THE CAPTAIN. Centurion.

THE CENTURION [*standing at attention and saluting*] Sir?

THE CAPTAIN [*speaking stiffly and officially*] You will remind your men, Centurion, that we are now entering Rome. You will instruct them that once inside the gates of Rome they are in the presence of the Emperor. You will make them understand that the lax discipline of the march cannot be permitted here. You will instruct them to shave every day, not every week. You will impress on them particularly that there must be an end to the profanity and blasphemy of singing Christian hymns on the march. I have to reprimand you, Centurion, for not only allowing this, but actually doing it yourself.

THE CENTURION [*apologetic*] The men march better, Captain.

THE CAPTAIN. No doubt. For that reason an exception is made in the case of the march called Onward Christian Soldiers. This may be sung, except when marching through the forum or within hearing of the Emperor's palace; but the words must be altered to "Throw them to the Lions."

The Christians burst into shrieks of uncontrollable laughter, to the great scandal of the Centurion.

CENTURION. Silence! Silen-n-n-nce! Wheres your behavior? Is that the way to listen to an officer? [*To the Captain*] Thats what we have to put up with from these Christians every day, sir. Theyre always laughing and joking something scandalous. Theyve no religion: thats how it is.

LAVINIA. But I think the Captain meant us to laugh, Centurion. It was so funny.

CENTURION. Youll find out how funny it is when youre thrown to the lions tomorrow. [*To the Captain, who looks displeased*] Beg pardon, Sir. [*To the Christians*] Silennnnce!

THE CAPTAIN. You are to instruct your men that all intimacy with Christian prisoners must now cease. The men have fallen into habits of dependence upon the prisoners, especially the female prisoners, for cooking, repairs to uniforms, writing letters, and advice in their private affairs. In a Roman soldier such dependence is inadmissible. Let me see no more of it whilst we are in the city. Further, your orders are that in addressing Christian prisoners, the manners and tone of your men must express abhorrence and contempt. Any shortcoming in this respect will be regarded as a breach of discipline. [*He turns to the prisoners*] Prisoners.

CENTURION [*fiercely*] Prisonerrrrrs! Tention! Silence!

THE CAPTAIN. I call your attention, prisoners, to the fact that you may be called on to appear in the Imperial Circus at any time from tomorrow onwards according to the requirements of the managers. I may inform you that as there is a shortage of Christians just now, you may expect to be called on very soon.

LAVINIA. What will they do to us, Captain?

CENTURION. Silence!

THE CAPTAIN. The women will be conducted into the arena with the wild beasts of the Imperial Menagerie, and will suffer the consequences. The men, if of an age to bear arms, will be given weapons to defend themselves, if they choose, against the Imperial Gladiators.

LAVINIA. Captain: is there no hope that this cruel persecution—

CENTURION [*shocked*] Silence! Hold your tongue, there. Persecution, indeed!

THE CAPTAIN [*unmoved and somewhat sardonic*] Persecution is not a term applicable to the acts of the Emperor. The Emperor is the Defender of the Faith. In throwing you to the lions he will be upholding the interests of religion in Rome. If you were to throw him to the lions, that would no doubt be persecution.

The Christians again laugh heartily.

CENTURION [*horrified*] Silence, I tell you! Keep silence there. Did anyone ever hear the like of this?

LAVINIA. Captain: there will be nobody to appreciate your jokes when we are gone.

THE CAPTAIN [*unshaken in his official delivery*] I call the attention of the female prisoner Lavinia to the fact that as the Emperor is a divine personage, her imputation of cruelty is not only treason, but sacrilege. I point out to her further that there is no foundation for the charge, as the Emperor does not desire that any prisoner should suffer; nor can any Christian be harmed save through his or her own obstinacy. All that is necessary is to sacrifice to the gods: a simple and convenient ceremony effected by dropping a pinch of incense on the altar, after which the prisoner is at once set free. Under such circumstances you have only your own perverse folly to blame if you suffer. I suggest to you that if you cannot burn a morsel of incense as a matter of conviction, you might at least do so as a matter of good taste, to avoid shocking the religious convictions of your fellow citizens. I am aware that these considerations do not weigh with Christians; but it is my duty to call your attention to them in order that you may have no ground for complaining of your treatment, or of accusing the Emperor of cruelty when he is shewing you the most signal clemency. Looked at from this point of view, every Christian who has perished in the arena has really committed suicide.

LAVINIA. Captain: your jokes are too grim. Do you think it is easy for us to die. Our faith makes life far stronger and more wonderful in us than when we walked in darkness and had nothing to live for. Death is harder for us than for you: the martyr's agony is as bitter as his triumph is glorious.

THE CAPTAIN [*rather troubled, addressing her personally and gravely*] A martyr, Lavinia, is a fool. Your death will prove nothing.

LAVINIA. Then why kill me?

THE CAPTAIN. I mean that truth, if there be any truth, needs no martyrs.

LAVINIA. No; but my faith, like your sword, needs testing. Can you test your sword except by staking your life on it?

THE CAPTAIN [*suddenly resuming his official tone*] I call the attention of the female prisoner to the fact that Christians are not allowed to draw the Emperor's officers into arguments and put questions to them for which the military regulations provide no answer. [*The Christians titter*].

LAVINIA. Captain: how can you?

THE CAPTAIN. I call the female prisoner's attention specially to the fact that four comfortable homes have been offered her by officers of this regiment, of which she can have her choice the moment she chooses to sacrifice as all wellbred Roman ladies do. I have no more to say to the prisoners.

CENTURION. Dismiss! But stay where you are.

THE CAPTAIN. Centurion: you will remain here with your men in charge of the prisoners until the arrival of three Christian prisoners in the custody of a cohort of the tenth legion. Among these prisoners you will particularly identify an armorer named Ferrovius, of dangerous character and great personal strength, and a Greek tailor reputed to be a sorcerer, by name Androcles. You will add the three to your charge here and march them all to the Coliseum, where you will deliver them into the custody of the master of the gladiators and take his receipt, countersigned by the keeper of the beasts and the acting manager. You understand your instructions?

CENTURION. Yes, sir.

THE CAPTAIN. Dismiss. [*He throws off his air of parade, and descends from his perch. The Centurion seats himself on it and prepares for a nap, whilst his men stand at ease. The Christians sit down on the west side of the square, glad to rest. Lavinia alone remains standing to speak to the Captain*].

LAVINIA. Captain: is this man who is to join us the famous Ferrovius, who has made such wonderful conversions in the northern cities?

THE CAPTAIN. Yes. We are warned that he has the strength of an elephant and the temper of a mad bull. Also that he is stark mad. Not a model Christian, it would seem.

LAVINIA. You need not fear him if he is a Christian, Captain.

THE CAPTAIN [*coldly*] I shall not fear him in any case, Lavinia.

LAVINIA [*her eyes dancing*] How brave of you, Captain!

THE CAPTAIN. You are right: it was a silly thing to say. [*In a lower tone, humane and urgent*] Lavinia: do Christians know how to love?

LAVINIA [*composedly*] Yes, Captain: they love even their enemies.

THE CAPTAIN. Is that easy?

LAVINIA. Very easy, Captain, when their enemies are as handsome as you.

THE CAPTAIN. Lavinia: you are laughing at me.

LAVINIA. At you, Captain! Impossible.

THE CAPTAIN. Then you are flirting with me, which is worse. Dont be foolish.

LAVINIA. But such a very handsome captain.

THE CAPTAIN. Incorrigible! [*Urgently*] Listen to me. The men in that audience tomorrow will be the vilest of voluptuaries: men in whom the only passion excited by a beautiful woman is a lust to see her tortured and torn shrieking limb from limb. It is a crime to gratify that passion. It is offering yourself for violation by the whole rabble of the streets and the riff-raff of the court at the same time. Why will you not choose rather a kindly love and an honorable alliance?

LAVINIA. They cannot violate my soul. I alone can do that by sacrificing to false gods.

THE CAPTAIN. Sacrifice then to the true God. What does his name matter? We call him Jupiter. The Greeks call him Zeus. Call him what you will as you drop the incense on the altar flame: He will understand.

LAVINIA. No. I couldnt. That is the strange thing, Captain, that a little pinch of incense should make all that difference. Religion is such a great thing that when I meet really religious people we are friends at once, no matter what name we give to the divine will that made us and moves us. Oh, do you think that I, a woman, would quarrel with you for sacrificing to a woman god like Diana, if Diana meant to you what Christ means to me? No: we should kneel side by side before her altar like two children. But when men who believe neither in my god nor in their own—men who do not know the meaning of the word religion —when these men drag me to the foot of an iron statue that has become the symbol of the terror and darkness through which they walk, of their cruelty and greed, of their hatred of God and their oppression of man—when they ask me to pledge my soul before the people that this hideous idol is God, and that all this wickedness and falsehood is divine truth, I cannot do it, not if they could put a thousand cruel deaths on me. I tell you, it is physically impossible. Listen, Captain: did you ever try to catch a mouse in your hand? Once there was a dear little mouse that used to come out and play on my table as I was reading. I wanted to take him in my hand and caress him; and sometimes he got among my books so that he could not escape me when I stretched out my hand. And I did stretch out my hand; but it always came back in spite of me. I was not afraid of him in my heart; but my hand refused: it is not in the nature of my hand to touch a mouse. Well, Captain, if I took a pinch of incense in my hand and stretched it out over the altar fire, my hand would come back. My body would be true to my faith even if you could corrupt my mind. And all the time I should believe more in Diana than my perse-cutors have ever believed in anything. Can you understand that?

THE CAPTAIN [*simply*] Yes: I understand that. But my hand would not come back. The hand that holds the sword has been trained not to come back from anything but victory.

LAVINIA. Not even from death?

THE CAPTAIN. Least of all from death.

LAVINIA. Then I must not come back from death either. A woman has to be braver than a soldier.

THE CAPTAIN. Prouder, you mean.

LAVINIA [*startled*] Prouder! You call our courage pride!

THE CAPTAIN. There is no such thing as courage: there is only pride. You Christians are the proudest devils on earth.

LAVINIA [*hurt*] Pray God then my pride may never become a false pride. [*She turns away as if she did not wish to continue the conversation, but softens and says to him with a smile*] Thank you for trying to save me.

THE CAPTAIN. I knew it was no use; but one tries in spite of one's knowledge.

LAVINIA. Something stirs, even in the iron breast of a Roman soldier?

THE CAPTAIN. It will soon be iron again. I have seen many women die, and forgotten them in a week.

LAVINIA. Remember me for a fortnight, handsome Captain. I shall be watching you, perhaps.

THE CAPTAIN. From the skies? Do not deceive yourself, Lavinia. There is no future for you beyond the grave.

LAVINIA. What does that matter? Do you think I am only running away from the terrors of life into the comfort of heaven? If there were no future, or if the future were one of torment, I should have to go just the same. The hand of God is upon me.

THE CAPTAIN. Yes: when all is said, we are both patricians, Lavinia, and must die for our beliefs. Farewell. [*He offers her his hand. She takes it and presses it. He walks away, trim and calm. She looks after him for a moment, and cries a little as he disappears through the eastern arch. A trumpet-call is heard from the road through the western arch*].

CENTURION [*waking up and rising*] Cohort of the tenth with prisoners. Two file out with me to receive them. [*He goes out through the western arch, followed by four soldiers in two files*].

Lentulus and Metellus come into the square from the west side with a little retinue of servants. Both are young courtiers, dressed in the extremity of fashion. Lentulus is slender, fair-haired, epicene. Metellus is manly, compactly built, olive skinned, not a talker.

LENTULUS. Christians, by Jove! Lets chaff them.

METELLUS. Awful brutes. If you knew as much about them as I do you wouldnt want to chaff them. Leave them to the lions.

LENTULUS [*indicating Lavinia, who is still looking towards the arches after the Captain*] That woman's got a figure. [*He walks past her, staring at her invitingly; but she is preoccupied and is not conscious of him*]. Do you turn the other cheek when they kiss you?

LAVINIA [*starting*] What?

LENTULUS. Do you turn the other cheek when they kiss you, fascinating Christian?

LAVINIA. Dont be foolish. [*To Metellus, who has remained on her right, so that she is between them*] Please dont let your friend behave like a cad before the soldiers. How are they to respect and obey patricians if they see them behaving like street boys? [*Sharply to Lentulus*] Pull yourself together, man. Hold your head up. Keep the corners of your mouth firm; and treat me respectfully. What do you take me for?

LENTULUS [*irresolutely*] Look here, you know: I—you—I—

LAVINIA. Stuff! Go about your business. [*She turns decisively away and sits down with her comrades, leaving him disconcertēd*].

METELLUS. You didnt get much out of that. I told you they were brutes.

LENTULUS. Plucky little filly! I suppose she thinks I care. [*With an air of indifference he strolls with Metellus to the east side of the square, where they stand watching the return of the Centurion through the western arch with his men, escorting three prisoners: Ferrovius, Androcles, and Spintho. Ferrovius is a powerful, choleric man in the prime of life, with large nostrils, stàring eyes, and a thick neck: a man whose sensibilities are keen and violent to the verge of madness. Spintho is a debauchee, the wreck of a good-looking man gone hopelessly to the bad. Androcles is overwhelmed with grief, and is restraining his tears with great difficulty*].

THE CENTURION [*to Lavinia*] Here are some pals for you. This little bit is Ferrovius that you talk so much about. [*Ferrovius turns on him threateningly. The Centurion holds up his left fore-finger in admonition*]. Now remember that youre a Christian, and that youve got to return good for evil. [*Ferrovius controls himself convulsively; moves away from temptation to the east side near Lentulus; clasps his hands in silent prayer; and throws himself on his knees*]. Thats the way to manage them, eh! This fine fellow

ANDROCLES AND THE LION

[*indicating Androcles, who comes to his left, and makes Lavinia a heart-broken salutation*] is a sorcerer. A Greek tailor, he is. A real sorcerer, too: no mistake about it. The tenth marches with a leopard at the head of the column. He made a pet of the leopard; and now he's crying at being parted from it. [*Androcles sniffs lamentably*]. Aint you, old chap? Well, cheer up, we march with a Billy goat [*Androcles brightens up*] thats killed two leopards and ate a turkey-cock. You can have him for a pet if you like. [*Androcles, quite consoled, goes past the Centurion to Lavinia, and sits down contentedly on the ground on her left*]. This dirty dog [*collaring Spintho*] is a real Christian. He mobs the temples, he does [*at each accusation he gives the neck of Spintho's tunic a twist*]; he goes smashing things mad drunk, he does; he steals the gold vessels, he does; he assaults the priestesses, he does—yah! [*He flings Spintho into the middle of the group of prisoners*]. Youre the sort that makes duty a pleasure, you are.

SPINTHO [*gasping*] Thats it: strangle me. Kick me. Beat me. Revile me. Our Lord was beaten and reviled. Thats my way to heaven. Every martyr goes to heaven, no matter what he's done. That is so, isnt it, brother?

CENTURION. Well, if youre going to heaven, *I* dont want to go there. I wouldnt be seen with you.

LENTULUS. Haw! Good! [*Indicating the kneeling Ferrovius*]. Is this one of the turn-the-other-cheek gentlemen, Centurion?

CENTURION. Yes, sir. Lucky for you too, sir, if you want to take any liberties with him.

LENTULUS [*to Ferrovius*] You turn the other cheek when youre struck, I'm told.

FERROVIUS [*slowly turning his great eyes on him*] Yes, by the grace of God, I do, n o w.

LENTULUS. Not that youre a coward, of course; but out of pure piety.

FERROVIUS. I fear God more than man; at least I try to.

LENTULUS. Lets see. [*He strikes him on the cheek. Androcles makes a wild movement to rise and interfere; but Lavinia holds him*

122

down, watching Ferrovius intently. Ferrovius, without flinching, turns the other cheek. Lentulus, rather out of countenance, titters foolishly, and strikes him again feebly]. You know, I should feel ashamed if I let myself be struck like that, and took it lying down. But then I'm not a Christian: I'm a man. [*Ferrovius rises impressively and towers over him. Lentulus becomes white with terror; and a shade of green flickers in his cheek for a moment*].

FERROVIUS [*with the calm of a steam hammer*] I have not always been faithful. The first man who struck me as you have just struck me was a stronger man than you: he hit me harder than I expected. I was tempted and fell; and it was then that I first tasted bitter shame. I never had a happy moment after that until I had knelt and asked his forgiveness by his bedside in the hospital. [*Putting his hands on Lentulus's shoulders with paternal weight*]. But now I have learnt to resist with a strength that is not my own. I am not ashamed now, nor angry.

LENTULUS [*uneasily*] Er—good evening. [*He tries to move away*].

FERROVIUS [*gripping his shoulders*] Oh, do not harden your heart, young man. Come: try for yourself whether our way is not better than yours. I will now strike you on one cheek; and you will turn the other and learn how much better you will feel than if you gave way to the promptings of anger. [*He holds him with one hand and clenches the other fist*].

LENTULUS. Centurion: I call on you to protect me.

CENTURION. You asked for it, sir. It's no business of ours. Youve had two whacks at him. Better pay him a trifle and square it that way.

LENTULUS. Yes, of course. [*To Ferrovius*] It was only a bit of fun, I assure you: I meant no harm. Here. [*He proffers a gold coin*].

FERROVIUS [*taking it and throwing it to the old beggar, who snatches it up eagerly, and hobbles off to spend it*] Give all thou hast to the poor. Come, friend: courage! I may hurt your body for a moment; but your soul will rejoice in the victory of the spirit over the flesh. [*He prepares to strike*].

ANDROCLES. Easy, Ferrovius, easy: you broke the last man's jaw.

Lentulus, with a moan of terror, attempts to fly; but Ferrovius holds him ruthlessly.

FERROVIUS. Yes; but I saved his soul. What matters a broken jaw?

LENTULUS. Dont touch me, do you hear? The law—

FERROVIUS. The law will throw me to the lions tomorrow: what worse could it do were I to slay you? Pray for strength; and it shall be given to you.

LENTULUS. Let me go. Your religion forbids you to strike me.

FERROVIUS. On the contrary, it commands me to strike you. How can you turn the other cheek, if you are not first struck on the one cheek?

LENTULUS [*almost in tears*] But I'm convinced already that what you said is quite right. I apologize for striking you.

FERROVIUS [*greatly pleased*] My son: have I softened your heart? Has the good seed fallen in a fruitful place? Are your feet turning towards a better path?

LENTULUS [*abjectly*] Yes, yes. Theres a great deal in what you say.

FERROVIUS [*radiant*] Join us. Come to the lions. Come to suffering and death.

LENTULUS [*falling on his knees and bursting into tears*] Oh, help me. Mother! mother!

FERROVIUS. These tears will water your soul and make it bring forth good fruit, my son. God has greatly blessed my efforts at conversion. Shall I tell you a miracle—yes, a miracle—wrought by me in Cappadocia? A young man—just such a one as you, with golden hair like yours—scoffed at and struck me as you scoffed at and struck me. I sat up all night with that youth wrestling for his soul; and in the morning not only was he a Christian, but his hair was as white as snow. [*Lentulus falls in a dead faint*]. There, there: take him away. The spirit has overwrought him, poor lad. Carry him gently to his house; and leave the rest to heaven.

CENTURION. Take him home. [*The servants, intimidated, hastily carry him out. Metellus is about to follow when Ferrovius lays his hand on his shoulder*].

FERROVIUS. You are his friend, young man. You will see that he is taken safely home.

METELLUS [*with awestruck civility*] Certainly, sir. I shall do whatever you think best. Most happy to have made your acquaintance, I'm sure. You may depend on me. Good evening, sir.

FERROVIUS [*with unction*] The blessing of heaven upon you and him.

Metellus follows Lentulus. The Centurion returns to his seat to resume his interrupted nap. The deepest awe has settled on the spectators. Ferrovius, with a long sigh of happiness, goes to Lavinia, and offers her his hand.

LAVINIA [*taking it*] So that is how you convert people, Ferrovius.

FERROVIUS. Yes: there has been a blessing on my work in spite of my unworthiness and my backslidings—all through my wicked, devilish temper. This man—

ANDROCLES [*hastily*] Dont slap me on the back, brother. She knows you mean me.

FERROVIUS. How I wish I were weak like our brother here! for then I should perhaps be meek and gentle like him. And yet there seems to be a special providence that makes my trials less than his. I hear tales of the crowd scoffing and casting stones and reviling the brethren; but when I come, all this stops: my influence calms the passions of the mob: they listen to me in silence; and infidels are often converted by a straight heart-to-heart talk with me. Every day I feel happier, more confident. Every day lightens the load of the great terror.

LAVINIA. The great terror? What is that?

Ferrovius shakes his head and does not answer. He sits down beside her on her left, and buries his face in his hands in gloomy meditation.

ANDROCLES. Well, you see, sister, he's never quite sure of himself. Suppose at the last moment in the arena, with the gladiators there to fight him, one of them was to say anything to annoy him, he might forget himself and lay that gladiator out.

LAVINIA. That would be splendid.

FERROVIUS [*springing up in horror*] What!

ANDROCLES. Oh, sister!

FERROVIUS. Splendid to betray my master, like Peter! Splendid to act like any common blackguard in the day of my proving! Woman: you are no Christian. [*He moves away from her to the middle of the square, as if her neighborhood contaminated him*].

LAVINIA [*laughing*] You know, Ferrovius, I am not always a Christian. I dont think anybody is. There are moments when I forget all about it, and something comes out quite naturally, as it did then.

SPINTHO. What does it matter? If you die in the arena, youll be a martyr; and all martyrs go to heaven, no matter what they have done. Thats so, isnt it, Ferrovius?

FERROVIUS. Yes: that is so, if we are faithful to the end.

LAVINIA. I'm not so sure.

SPINTHO. Dont say that. Thats blasphemy. Dont say that, I tell you. We shall be saved, no matter WHAT we do.

LAVINIA. Perhaps you men will all go into heaven bravely and in triumph, with your heads erect and golden trumpets sounding for you. But I am sure I shall only be allowed to squeeze myself in through a little crack in the gate after a great deal of begging. I am not good always: I have moments only.

SPINTHO. Youre talking nonsense, woman. I tell you, martyrdom pays all scores.

ANDROCLES. Well, let us hope so, brother, for your sake. Youve had a gay time, havnt you? with your raids on the temples. I cant help thinking that heaven will be very dull for a man of your temperament. [*Spintho snarls*]. Dont be angry: I say it only to console you in case you should die in your bed tonight in the natural way. Theres a lot of plague about.

SPINTHO [*rising and running about in abject terror*] I never thought of that. Oh Lord, spare me to be martyred. Oh, what a thought to put into the mind of a brother! Oh, let me be martyred today, now. I shall die in the night and go to hell. Youre a sorcerer: youve put death into my mind. Oh, curse you, curse you! [*He tries to seize Androcles by the throat*].

FERROVIUS [*holding him in a grasp of iron*] Whats this, brother? Anger! Violence! Raising your hand to a brother Christian!

SPINTHO. It's easy for you. Youre strong. Your nerves are all right. But I'm full of disease. [*Ferrovius takes his hand from him with instinctive disgust*]. Ive drunk all my nerves away. I shall have the horrors all night.

ANDROCLES [*sympathetic*] Oh, dont take on so, brother. We're all sinners.

SPINTHO [*snivelling, trying to feel consoled*] Yes: I daresay if the truth were known, youre all as bad as I am.

LAVINIA [*contemptuously*] Does that comfort you?

FERROVIUS [*sternly*] Pray, man, pray.

SPINTHO. Whats the good of praying? If we're martyred we shall go to heaven, shant we, whether we pray or not?

FERROVIUS. Whats that? Not pray! [*Seizing him again*] Pray this instant, you dog, you rotten hound, you slimy snake, you beastly goat, or—

SPINTHO. Yes: beat me: kick me. I forgive you: mind that.

FERROVIUS [*spurning him with loathing*] Yah! [*Spintho reels away and falls in front of Ferrovius*].

ANDROCLES [*reaching out and catching the skirt of Ferrovius's tunic*] Dear brother: if you wouldnt mind—just for my sake—

FERROVIUS. Well?

ANDROCLES. Dont call him by the names of the animals. Weve no right to. Ive had such friends in dogs. A pet snake is the best of company. I was nursed on goat's milk. Is it fair to them to call the like of him a dog or a snake or a goat?

I

FERROVIUS. I only meant that they have no souls.

ANDROCLES [*anxiously protesting*] Oh, believe me, they have. Just the same as you and me. I really dont think I could consent to go to heaven if I thought there were to be no animals there. Think of what they suffer here.

FERROVIUS. Thats true. Yes: that is just. They will have their share in heaven.

SPINTHO [*who has picked himself up and is sneaking past Ferrovius on his left, sneers derisively*]!!

FERROVIUS [*turning on him fiercely*] Whats that you say?

SPINTHO [*cowering*] Nothing.

FERROVIUS [*clenching his fist*] Do animals go to heaven or not?

SPINTHO. I never said they didnt.

FERROVIUS [*implacable*] Do they or do they not?

SPINTHO. They do: they do. [*Scrambling out of Ferrovius's reach*]. Oh, curse you for frightening me!

A bugle call is heard.

CENTURION [*waking up*] Tention! Form as before. Now then, prisoners: up with you and trot along spry. [*The soldiers fall in. The Christians rise*].

A man with an ox goad comes running through the central arch.

THE OX DRIVER. Here, you soldiers! clear out of the way for the Emperor.

THE CENTURION. Emperor! Where's the Emperor? You aint the Emperor, are you?

THE OX DRIVER. It's the menagerie service. My team of oxen is drawing the new lion to the Coliseum. You clear the road.

CENTURION. What! Go in after you in your dust, with half the town at the heels of you and your lion! Not likely. We go first.

THE OX DRIVER. The menagerie service is the Emperor's personal retinue. You clear out, I tell you.

CENTURION. You tell me, do you? Well, I'll tell you something. If the lion is menagerie service, the lion's dinner is menagerie service too. This [*pointing to the Christians*] is the lion's dinner. So back with you to your bullocks double quick;

and learn your place. March. [*The soldiers start*]. Now then, you Christians: step out there.

LAVINIA [*marching*] Come along, the rest of the dinner. I shall be the olives and anchovies.

ANOTHER CHRISTIAN [*laughing*] I shall be the soup.

ANOTHER. I shall be the fish.

ANOTHER. Ferrovius shall be the roast boar.

FERROVIUS [*heavily*] I see the joke. Yes, yes: I shall be the roast boar. Ha! ha! [*He laughs conscientiously and marches out with them*].

ANDROCLES [*following*] I shall be the mince pie. [*Each announcement is received with a louder laugh by all the rest as the joke catches on*].

CENTURION [*scandalized*] Silence! Have some sense of your situation. Is this the way for martyrs to behave? [*To Spintho, who is quaking and loitering*] I know what youll be at that dinner. Youll be the emetic. [*He shoves him rudely along*].

SPINTHO. It's too dreadful: I'm not fit to die.

CENTURION. Fitter than you are to live, you swine.

They pass from the square westward. The oxen, drawing a waggon with a great wooden cage and the lion in it, arrive through the central arch.

ACT II

Behind the Emperor's box at the Coliseum, where the performers assemble before entering the arena. In the middle a wide passage leading to the arena descends from the floor level under the imperial box. On both sides of this passage steps ascend to a landing at the back entrance to the box. The landing forms a bridge across the passage. At the entrance to the passage are two bronze mirrors, one on each side.

On the west side of this passage, on the right hand of anyone coming from the box and standing on the bridge, the martyrs are sitting on the steps. Lavinia is seated half-way up, thoughtful, trying to look death in the face. On her left Androcles consoles himself by nursing a cat. Ferrovius stands behind them, his eyes blazing, his figure stiff with intense resolution. At the foot of the steps crouches Spintho, with his head clutched in his hands, full of horror at the approach of martyrdom.

On the east side of the passage the gladiators are standing and sitting at ease, waiting, like the Christians, for their turn in the arena. One (Retiarius) is a nearly naked man with a net and a trident. Another (Secutor) is in armor with a sword. He carries a helmet with a barred visor. The editor of the gladiators sits on a chair a little apart from them.

The Call Boy enters from the passage.

THE CALL BOY. Number six. Retiarius versus Secutor.

The gladiator with the net picks it up. The gladiator with the helmet puts it on; and the two go into the arena, the net thrower taking out a little brush and arranging his hair as he goes, the other tightening his straps and shaking his shoulders loose. Both look at themselves in the mirrors before they enter the passage.

LAVINIA. Will they really kill one another?

SPINTHO. Yes, if the people turn down their thumbs.

THE EDITOR. You know nothing about it. The people indeed! Do you suppose we would kill a man worth perhaps fifty talents

130

to please the riffraff ? I should like to catch any of my men at it.

SPINTHO. I thought—

THE EDITOR [*contemptuously*] You thought! Who cares what you think? Youll be killed all right enough.

SPINTHO [*groans and again hides his face*]!!!

LAVINIA. Then is nobody ever killed except us poor Christians?

THE EDITOR. If the vestal virgins turn down their thumbs, thats another matter. Theyre ladies of rank.

LAVINIA. Does the Emperor ever interfere?

THE EDITOR. Oh, yes: he turns his thumb up fast enough if the vestal virgins want to have one of his pet fighting men killed.

ANDROCLES. But dont they ever just only pretend to kill one another? Why shouldnt you pretend to die, and get dragged out as if you were dead; and then get up and go home, like an actor?

THE EDITOR. See here: you want to know too much. There will be no pretending about the new lion: let that be enough for you. He's hungry.

SPINTHO [*groaning with horror*] Oh, Lord! cant you stop talking about it? Isnt it bad enough for us without that?

ANDROCLES. I'm glad he's hungry. Not that I want him to suffer, poor chap! but then he'll enjoy eating me so much more. Theres a cheerful side to everything.

THE EDITOR [*rising and striding over to Androcles*] Here: dont you be obstinate. Come with me and drop the pinch of incense on the altar. Thats all you need do to be let off.

ANDROCLES. No: thank you very much indeed; but I really mustnt.

THE EDITOR. What! Not to save your life?

ANDROCLES. I'd rather not. I couldnt sacrifice to Diana: she's a huntress, you know, and kills things.

THE EDITOR. That dont matter. You can choose your own altar. Sacrifice to Jupiter: he likes animals: he turns himself into an animal when he goes off duty.

ANDROCLES. No: it's very kind of you; but I feel I cant save myself that way.

THE EDITOR. But I dont ask you to do it to save yourself: I ask you to do it to oblige me personally.

ANDROCLES [*scrambling up in the greatest agitation*] Oh, please dont say that. This is dreadful. You mean so kindly by me that it seems quite horrible to disoblige you. If you could arrange for me to sacrifice when theres nobody looking, I shouldnt mind. But I must go into the arena with the rest. My honor, you know.

THE EDITOR. Honor! The honor of a tailor?

ANDROCLES [*apologetically*] Well, perhaps honor is too strong an expression. Still, you know, I couldnt allow the tailors to get a bad name through me.

THE EDITOR. How much will you remember of all that when you smell the beast's breath and see his jaws opening to tear out your throat?

SPINTHO [*rising with a yell of terror*] I cant bear it. Wheres the altar? I'll sacrifice.

FERROVIUS. Dog of an apostate. Iscariot!

SPINTHO. I'll repent afterwards. I fully mean to die in the arena: I'll die a martyr and go to heaven; but not this time, not now, not until my nerves are better. Besides, I'm too young: I want to have just one more good time. [*The gladiators laugh at him*]. Oh, will no one tell me where the altar is? [*He dashes into the passage and vanishes*].

ANDROCLES [*to the Editor, pointing after Spintho*] Brother: I cant do that, not even to oblige you. Dont ask me.

THE EDITOR. Well, if youre determined to die, I cant help you. But I wouldnt be put off by a swine like that.

FERROVIUS. Peace, peace: tempt him not. Get thee behind him, Satan.

THE EDITOR [*flushing with rage*] For two pins I'd take a turn in the arena myself today, and pay you out for daring to talk to me like that.

Ferrovius springs forward.

LAVINIA [*rising quickly and interposing*] Brother, brother: you forget.

FERROVIUS [*curbing himself by a mighty effort*] Oh, my temper, my wicked temper! [*To the Editor, as Lavinia sits down again, reassured*] Forgive me, brother. My heart was full of wrath: I should have been thinking of your dear precious soul.

THE EDITOR. Yah! [*He turns his back on Ferrovius contemptuously, and goes back to his seat*].

FERROVIUS [*continuing*] And I forgot it all: I thought of nothing but offering to fight you with one hand tied behind me.

THE EDITOR [*turning pugnaciously*] What!

FERROVIUS [*on the border line between zeal and ferocity*] Oh, dont give way to pride and wrath, brother. I could do it so easily. I could—

They are separated by the Menagerie Keeper, who rushes in from the passage, furious.

THE KEEPER. Heres a nice business! Who let that Christian out of here down to the dens when we were changing the lion into the cage next the arena?

THE EDITOR. Nobody let him. He let himself.

THE KEEPER. Well, the lion's ate him.

Consternation. The Christians rise, greatly agitated. The gladiators sit callously, but are highly amused. All speak or cry out or laugh at once. Tumult.

LAVINIA. Oh, poor wretch! FERROVIUS. The apostate has perished. Praise be to God's justice! ANDROCLES. The poor beast was starving. It couldnt help itself. THE CHRISTIANS. What! Ate him! How frightful! How terrible! Without a moment to repent! God be merciful to him, a sinner! Oh, I cant bear to think of it! In the midst of his sin! Horrible, horrible! THE EDITOR. Serve the rotter right! THE GLADIATORS. Just walked into it, he did. He's martyred all right enough. Good old lion! Old Jock doesn't like that: look at his face. Devil a better! The Emperor will laugh when he hears of it. I cant help smiling. Ha ha ha!!!!!

THE KEEPER. Now his appetite's taken off, he wont as much as look at another Christian for a week.

ANDROCLES. Couldnt you have saved him, brother?

ANDROCLES AND THE LION

THE KEEPER. Saved him! Saved him from a lion that I'd just got mad with hunger! a wild one that came out of the forest not four weeks ago! He bolted him before you could say Balbus.

LAVINIA [*sitting down again*] Poor Spintho! And it wont even count as martyrdom!

THE KEEPER. Serve him right! What call had he to walk down the throat of one of my lions before he was asked?

ANDROCLES. Perhaps the lion wont eat me now.

THE KEEPER. Yes: thats just like a Christian: think only of yourself! What am *I* to do? What am I to say to the Emperor when he sees one of my lions coming into the arena half asleep?

THE EDITOR. Say nothing. Give your old lion some bitters and a morsel of fried fish to wake up his appetite. [*Laughter*].

THE KEEPER. Yes: it's easy for you to talk; but—

THE EDITOR [*scrambling to his feet*] Sh! Attention there! The Emperor. [*The Keeper bolts precipitately into the passage. The gladiators rise smartly and form into line*].

The Emperor enters on the Christians' side, conversing with Metellus, and followed by his suite.

THE GLADIATORS. Hail, Caesar! those about to die salute thee.

CAESAR. Good morrow, friends.

Metellus shakes hands with the Editor, who accepts his condescension with bluff respect.

LAVINIA. Blessing, Caesar, and forgiveness!

CAESAR [*turning in some surprise at the salutation*] There is no forgiveness for Christianity.

LAVINIA. I did not mean that, Caesar. I mean that we forgive you.

METELLUS. An inconceivable liberty! Do you not know, woman, that the Emperor can do no wrong and therefore cannot be forgiven?

LAVINIA. I expect the Emperor knows better. Anyhow, we forgive him.

THE CHRISTIANS. Amen!

CAESAR. Metellus: you see now the disadvantage of too much

severity. These people have no hope; therefore they have nothing to restrain them from saying what they like to me. They are almost as impertinent as the gladiators. Which is the Greek sorcerer?

ANDROCLES [*humbly touching his forelock*] Me, your Worship.

CAESAR. My Worship! Good! A new title. Well: what miracles can you perform?

ANDROCLES. I can cure warts by rubbing them with my tailor's chalk; and I can live with my wife without beating her.

CAESAR. Is that all?

ANDROCLES. You dont know her, Caesar, or you wouldnt say that.

CAESAR. Ah, well, my friend, we shall no doubt contrive a happy release for you. Which is Ferrovius?

FERROVIUS. I am he.

CAESAR. They tell me you can fight.

FERROVIUS. It is easy to fight. *I* can die, Caesar.

CAESAR. That is still easier, is it not?

FERROVIUS. Not to me, Caesar. Death comes hard to my flesh; and fighting comes very easily to my spirit [*beating his breast and lamenting*] Oh, sinner that I am! [*He throws himself down on the steps, deeply discouraged*].

CAESAR. Metellus: I should like to have this man in the Pretorian Guard.

METELLUS. *I* should not, Caesar. He looks a spoilsport. There are men in whose presence it is impossible to have any fun: men who are a sort of walking conscience. He would make us all uncomfortable.

CAESAR. For that reason, perhaps, it might be as well to have him. An Emperor can hardly have too many consciences. [*To Ferrovius*] Listen, Ferrovius. [*Ferrovius shakes his head and will not look up*]. You and your friends shall not be outnumbered today in the arena. You shall have arms; and there will be no more than one gladiator to each Christian. If you come out of the arena alive, I will consider favorably any request of yours, and give you a place in the Pretorian Guard. Even if the request be that no questions be asked about your faith I shall perhaps not refuse it.

FERROVIUS. I will not fight. I will die. Better stand with the archangels than with the Pretorian Guard.

CAESAR. I cannot believe that the archangels—whoever they may be—would not prefer to be recruited from the Pretorian Guard. However, as you please. Come: let us see the show.

As the Court ascends the steps, Secutor and Retiarius return from the arena through the passage: Secutor covered with dust and very angry: Retiarius grinning.

SECUTOR. Ha, the Emperor. Now we shall see. Caesar: I ask you whether it is fair for the Retiarius, instead of making a fair throw of his net at me, to swish it along the ground and throw the dust in my eyes, and then catch me when I'm blinded. If the vestals had not turned up their thumbs I should have been a dead man.

CAESAR [*halting on the stair*] There is nothing in the rules against it.

SECUTOR [*indignantly*] Caesar: is it a dirty trick or is it not?

CAESAR. It is a dusty one, my friend. [*Obsequious laughter*]. Be on your guard next time.

SECUTOR. Let him be on his guard. Next time I'll throw my sword at his heels and strangle him with his own net before he can hop off. [*To the Retiarius*] You see if I dont. [*He goes out past the gladiators, sulky and furious*].

CAESAR [*to the chuckling Retiarius*] These tricks are not wise, my friend. The audience likes to see a dead man in all his beauty and splendor. If you smudge his face and spoil his armor they will shew their displeasure by not letting you kill him. And when your turn comes, they will remember it against you and turn their thumbs down.

THE RETIARIUS. Perhaps that is why I did it, Caesar. He bet me ten sesterces that he would vanquish me. If I had had to kill him I should not have had the money.

CAESAR [*indulgent, laughing*] You rogues: there is no end to your tricks. I'll dismiss you all and have elephants to fight. They fight fairly. [*He goes up to his box, and knocks at it. It is opened from within by the Captain, who stands as on parade to let him pass*].

The Call Boy comes from the passage, followed by three attendants carrying respectively a bundle of swords, some helmets, and some breastplates and pieces of armor which they throw down in a heap.

THE CALL BOY. By your leave, Caesar. Number eleven! Gladiators and Christians!

Ferrovius springs up, ready for martyrdom. The other Christians take the summons as best they can, some joyful and brave, some patient and dignified, some tearful and helpless, some embracing one another with emotion. The Call Boy goes back into the passage.

CAESAR [*turning at the door of the box*] The hour has come, Ferrovius. I shall go into my box and see you killed, since you scorn the Pretorian Guard. [*He goes into the box. The Captain shuts the door, remaining inside with the Emperor, Metellus and the rest of the suite disperse to their seats. The Christians, led by Ferrovius, move towards the passage*].

LAVINIA [*to Ferrovius*] Farewell.

THE EDITOR. Steady there. You Christians have got to fight. Here! arm yourselves.

FERROVIUS [*picking up a sword*] I'll die sword in hand to shew people that I could fight if it were my Master's will, and that I could kill the man who kills me if I chose.

THE EDITOR. Put on that armor.

FERROVIUS. No armor.

THE EDITOR [*bullying him*] Do what youre told. Put on that armor.

FERROVIUS [*gripping the sword and looking dangerous*] I said, No armor.

THE EDITOR. And what am I to say when I am accused of sending a naked man in to fight my men in armor?

FERROVIUS. Say your prayers, brother; and have no fear of the princes of this world.

THE EDITOR. Tsha! You obstinate fool! [*He bites his lips irresolutely, not knowing exactly what to do*].

ANDROCLES [*to Ferrovius*] Farewell, brother, till we meet in the sweet by-and-by.

THE EDITOR [*to Androcles*] You are going too. Take a sword there; and put on any armor you can find to fit you.

ANDROCLES. No, really: I cant fight: I never could: I cant bring myself to dislike anyone enough. I'm to be thrown to the lions with the lady.

THE EDITOR. Then get out of the way and hold your noise. [*Androcles steps aside with cheerful docility*]. Now then! Are you all ready there?

A trumpet is heard from the arena.

FERROVIUS [*starting convulsively*] Heaven give me strength!

THE EDITOR. Aha! That frightens you, does it?

FERROVIUS. Man: there is no terror like the terror of that sound to me. When I hear a trumpet or a drum or the clash of steel or the hum of the catapult as the great stone flies, fire runs through my veins: I feel my blood surge up hot behind my eyes: I must charge: I must strike: I must conquer: Caesar himself will not be safe in his imperial seat if once that spirit gets loose in me. Oh, brothers, pray! exhort me! remind me that if I raise my sword my honor falls and my Master is crucified afresh.

ANDROCLES. Just keep thinking how cruelly you might hurt the poor gladiators.

FERROVIUS. It does not hurt a man to kill him.

LAVINIA. Nothing but faith can save you.

FERROVIUS. Faith! Which faith? There are two faiths. There is our faith. And there is the warrior's faith, the faith in fighting, the faith that sees God in the sword. How if that faith should overwhelm me?

LAVINIA. You will find your real faith in the hour of trial.

FERROVIUS. That is what I fear. I know that I am a fighter. How can I feel sure that I am a Christian?

ANDROCLES. Throw away the sword, brother.

FERROVIUS. I cannot. It cleaves to my hand. I could as easily throw a woman I loved from my arms. [*Starting*] Who spoke that blasphemy? Not I.

LAVINIA. I cant help you, friend. I cant tell you not to save your own life. Something wilful in me wants to see you fight your way into heaven.

FERROVIUS. Ha!

ANDROCLES. But if you are going to give up our faith, brother, why not do it without hurting anybody? Dont fight them. Burn the incense.

FERROVIUS. Burn the incense! Never.

LAVINIA. That is only pride, Ferrovius.

FERROVIUS. Only pride! What is nobler than pride? [*Conscience stricken*] Oh, I'm steeped in sin. I'm proud of my pride.

LAVINIA. They say we Christians are the proudest devils on earth—that only the weak are meek. Oh, I am worse than you. I ought to send you to death; and I am tempting you.

ANDROCLES. Brother, brother: let them rage and kill: let us be brave and suffer. You must go as a lamb to the slaughter.

FERROVIUS. Aye, aye: that is right. Not as a lamb is slain by the butcher; but as a butcher might let himself be slain by a [*looking at the Editor*] by a silly ram whose head he could fetch off in one twist.

Before the Editor can retort, the Call Boy rushes up through the passage, and the Captain comes from the Emperor's box and descends the steps.

THE CALL BOY. In with you: into the arena. The stage is waiting.

THE CAPTAIN. The Emperor is waiting. [*To the Editor*] What are you dreaming of, man? Send your men in at once.

THE EDITOR. Yes, sir: it's these Christians hanging back.

FERROVIUS [*in a voice of thunder*] Liar!

THE EDITOR [*not heeding him*] March. [*The gladiators told off to fight with the Christians march down the passage*] Follow up there, you.

THE CHRISTIAN MEN AND WOMEN [*as they part*] Be steadfast,

brother. Farewell. Hold up the faith, brother. Farewell. Go to glory, dearest. Farewell. Remember: we are praying for you. Farewell. Be strong, brother. Farewell. Dont forget that the divine love and our love surround you. Farewell. Nothing can hurt you: remember that, brother. Farewell. Eternal glory, dearest. Farewell.

THE EDITOR [*out of patience*] Shove them in, there.

The remaining gladiators and the Call Boy make a movement towards them.

FERROVIUS [*interposing*] Touch them, dogs; and we die here, and cheat the heathen of their spectacle. [*To his fellow Christians*] Brothers: the great moment has come. That passage is your hill to Calvary. Mount it bravely, but meekly; and remember! not a word of reproach, not a blow nor a struggle. Go. [*They go out through the passage. He turns to Lavinia*] Farewell.

LAVINIA. You forget: I must follow before you are cold.

FERROVIUS. It is true. Do not envy me because I pass before you to glory. [*He goes through the passage*].

THE EDITOR [*to the Call Boy*] Sickening work, this. Why cant they all be thrown to the lions? It's not a man's job. [*He throws himself moodily into his chair*].

The remaining gladiators go back to their former places indifferently. The Call Boy shrugs his shoulders and squats down at the entrance to the passage, near the Editor.

Lavinia and the Christian women sit down again, wrung with grief, some weeping silently, some praying, some calm and steadfast. Androcles sits down at Lavinia's feet. The Captain stands on the stairs, watching her curiously.

ANDROCLES. I'm glad I havnt to fight. That would really be an awful martyrdom. I am lucky.

LAVINIA [*looking at him with a pang of remorse*] Androcles: burn the incense: youll be forgiven. Let my death atone for both. I feel as if I were killing you.

ANDROCLES. Dont think of me, sister. Think of yourself. That will keep your heart up.

The Captain laughs sardonically.

LAVINIA [*startled: she had forgotten his presence*] Are you there, handsome Captain? Have you come to see me die?

THE CAPTAIN [*coming to her side*] I am on duty with the Emperor, Lavinia.

LAVINIA. Is it part of your duty to laugh at us?

THE CAPTAIN. No: that is part of my private pleasure. Your friend here is a humorist. I laughed at his telling you to think of yourself to keep up your heart. *I* say, think of yourself and burn the incense.

LAVINIA. He is not a humorist: he was right. You ought to know that, Captain: you have been face to face with death.

THE CAPTAIN. Not with certain death, Lavinia. Only death in battle, which spares more men than death in bed. What you are facing is certain death. You have nothing left now but your faith in this craze of yours: this Christianity. Are your Christian fairy stories any truer than our stories about Jupiter and Diana, in which, I may tell you, I believe no more than the Emperor does, or any educated man in Rome?

LAVINIA. Captain: all that seems nothing to me now. I'll not say that death is a terrible thing; but I will say that it is so real a thing that when it comes close, all the imaginary things—all the stories, as you call them—fade into mere dreams beside that inexorable reality. I know now that I am not dying for stories or dreams. Did you hear of the dreadful thing that happened here while we were waiting?

THE CAPTAIN. I heard that one of your fellows bolted, and ran right into the jaws of the lion. I laughed. I still laugh.

LAVINIA. Then you dont understand what that meant?

THE CAPTAIN. It meant that the lion had a cur for his breakfast.

LAVINIA. It meant more than that, Captain. It meant that a man cannot die for a story and a dream. None of us believed the stories and the dreams more devoutly than poor Spintho; but he could not face the great reality. What he would have called my faith has been oozing away minute by minute whilst Ive been

141

sitting here, with death coming nearer and nearer, with reality becoming realler and realler, with stories and dreams fading away into nothing.

THE CAPTAIN. Are you then going to die for nothing?

LAVINIA. Yes: that is the wonderful thing. It is since all the stories and dreams have gone that I have now no doubt at all that I must die for something greater than dreams or stories.

THE CAPTAIN. But for what?

LAVINIA. I dont know. If it were for anything small enough to know, it would be too small to die for. I think I'm going to die for God. Nothing else is real enough to die for.

THE CAPTAIN. What is God?

LAVINIA. When we know that, Captain, we shall be gods ourselves.

THE CAPTAIN. Lavinia: come down to earth. Burn the incense and marry me.

LAVINIA. Handsome Captain: would you marry me if I hauled down the flag in the day of battle and burnt the incense? Sons take after their mothers, you know. Do you want your son to be a coward?

THE CAPTAIN [*strongly moved*] By great Diana, I think I would strangle you if you gave in now.

LAVINIA [*putting her hand on the head of Androcles*] The hand of God is on us three, Captain.

THE CAPTAIN. What nonsense it all is! And what a monstrous thing that you should die for such nonsense, and that I should look on helplessly when my whole soul cries out against it! Die then if you must; but at least I can cut the Emperor's throat and then my own when I see your blood.

The Emperor throws open the door of his box angrily, and appears in wrath on the threshold. The Editor, the Call Boy, and the gladiators spring to their feet.

THE EMPEROR. The Christians will not fight, and your curs cannot get their blood up to attack them. It's all that fellow with the blazing eyes. Send for the whip. [*The Call Boy rushes out on the east side for the whip*]. If that will not move them, bring the hot irons. The man is like a mountain. [*He returns angrily into the box and slams the door*].

The Call Boy returns with a man in a hideous Etruscan mask, carrying a whip. They both rush down the passage into the arena.

LAVINIA [*rising*] Oh, that is unworthy. Can they not kill him without dishonoring him?

ANDROCLES [*scrambling to his feet and running into the middle of the space between the staircases*] It's dreadful. Now *I* want to fight. I cant bear the sight of a whip. The only time I ever hit a man was when he lashed an old horse with a whip. It was terrible: I danced on his face when he was on the ground. He mustnt strike Ferrovius: I'll go into the arena and kill him first. [*He makes a wild dash into the passage. As he does so a great clamor is heard from the arena, ending in wild applause. The gladiators listen and look inquiringly at one another*].

THE EDITOR. Whats up now?

LAVINIA [*to the Captain*] What has happened, do you think?

THE CAPTAIN. What can happen? They are killing them, I suppose.

ANDROCLES [*running in through the passage, screaming with horror and hiding his eyes*]!!!

LAVINIA. Androcles, Androcles: whats the matter?

ANDROCLES. Oh dont ask me, dont ask me. Something too dreadful. Oh! [*He crouches by her and hides his face in her robe, sobbing*].

THE CALL BOY [*rushing through from the passage as before*] Ropes and hooks there! Ropes and hooks!

THE EDITOR. Well, need you excite yourself about it? [*Another burst of applause*].

Two slaves in Etruscan masks, with ropes and drag hooks, hurry in.

ONE OF THE SLAVES. How many dead?

THE CALL BOY. Six. [*The slave blows a whistle twice; and four more masked slaves rush through into the arena with the same*

K

apparatus]. And the basket. Bring the baskets. [*The slave whistles three times, and runs through the passage with his companion*].

THE CAPTAIN. Who are the baskets for?

THE CALL BOY. For the whip. He's in pieces. Theyre all in pieces, more or less. [*Lavinia hides her face*].

Two more masked slaves come in with a basket and follow the others into the arena, as the Call Boy turns to the gladiators and exclaims, exhausted, Boys: he's killed the lot.

THE EMPEROR [*again bursting from his box, this time in an ecstasy of delight*] Where is he? Magnificent! He shall have a laurel crown.

Ferrovius, madly waving his bloodstained sword, rushes through the passage in despair, followed by his co-religionists, and by the menagerie keeper, who goes to the gladiators. The gladiators draw their swords nervously.

FERROVIUS. Lost! lost for ever! I have betrayed my Master. Cut off this right hand: it has offended. Ye have swords, my brethren: strike.

LAVINIA. No, no. What have you done, Ferrovius?

FERROVIUS. I know not; but there was blood behind my eyes; and theres blood on my sword. What does that mean?

THE EMPEROR [*enthusiastically, on the landing outside his box*] What does it mean? It means that you are the greatest man in Rome. It means that you shall have a laurel crown of gold. Superb fighter: I could almost yield you my throne. It is a record for my reign: I shall live in history. Once, in Domitian's time, a Gaul slew three men in the arena and gained his freedom. But when before has one naked man slain six armed men of the bravest and best? The persecution shall cease: if Christians can fight like this, I shall have none but Christians to fight for me. [*To the Gladiators*] You are ordered to become Christians, you there: do you hear?

RETIARIUS. It is all one to us, Caesar. Had I been there with my net, the story would have been different.

THE CAPTAIN [*suddenly seizing Lavinia by the wrist and dragging her up the steps to the Emperor*] Caesar: this woman is the sister of Ferrovius. If she is thrown to the lions he will fret. He will lose weight; get out of condition—

THE EMPEROR. The lions? Nonsense! [*To Lavinia*] Madam: I am proud to have the honor of making your acquaintance. Your brother is the glory of Rome.

LAVINIA. But my friends here. Must they die?

THE EMPEROR. Die! Certainly not. There has never been the slightest idea of harming them. Ladies and gentlemen: you are all free. Pray go into the front of the house and enjoy the spectacle to which your brother has so splendidly contributed. Captain: oblige me by conducting them to the seats reserved for my personal friends.

THE MENAGERIE KEEPER. Caesar: I must have one Christian for the lion. The people have been promised it; and they will tear the decorations to bits if they are disappointed.

THE EMPEROR. True, true: we must have somebody for the new lion.

FERROVIUS. Throw me to him. Let the apostate perish.

THE EMPEROR. No, no: you would tear him in pieces, my friend; and we cannot afford to throw away lions as if they were mere slaves. But we must have somebody. This is really extremely awkward.

THE MENAGERIE KEEPER. Why not that little Greek chap? He's not a Christian: he's a sorcerer.

THE EMPEROR. The very thing: he will do very well.

THE CALL BOY [*issuing from the passage*] Number twelve. The Christian for the new lion.

ANDROCLES [*rising, and pulling himself sadly together*] Well, it was to be, after all.

LAVINIA. I'll go in his place, Caesar. Ask the Captain whether they do not like best to see a woman torn to pieces. He told me so yesterday.

THE EMPEROR. There is something in that: there is certainly something in that—if only I could feel sure that your brother would not fret.

ANDROCLES. No: I should never have another happy hour. No: on the faith of a Christian and the honor of a tailor, I accept the lot that has fallen on me. If my wife turns up, give her my love and say that my wish was that she should be happy with her next, poor fellow! Caesar: go to your box and see how a tailor can die. Make way for number twelve there. [*He marches out along the passage*].

The vast audience in the amphitheatre now sees the Emperor reenter his box and take his place as Androcles, desperately frightened, but still marching with piteous devotion, emerges from the other end of the passage, and finds himself at the focus of thousands of eager eyes. The lion's cage, with a heavy portcullis grating, is on his left. The Emperor gives a signal. A gong sounds. Androcles shivers at the sound; then falls on his knees and prays. The grating rises with a clash. The lion bounds into the arena. He rushes round frisking in his freedom. He sees Androcles. He stops; rises stiffly by straightening his legs; stretches out his nose forward and his tail in a horizontal line behind, like a pointer, and utters an appalling roar. Androcles crouches and hides his face in his hands. The lion gathers himself for a spring, swishing his tail to and fro through the dust in an ecstasy of anticipation. Androcles throws up his hands in supplication to heaven. The lion checks at the sight of Androcles's face. He then steals towards him; smells him; arches his back; purrs like a motor car; finally rubs himself against Androcles, knocking him over. Androcles, supporting himself on his wrist, looks affrightedly at the lion. The lion limps on three paws, holding up the other as if it was wounded. A flash of recognition lights up the face of Androcles. He flaps his hand as if it had a thorn in it, and pretends to pull the thorn out and to hurt himself. The lion nods repeatedly. Androcles holds out his hands to the lion, who gives him both paws, which he shakes with enthusiasm. They embrace rapturously, finally waltz round the arena amid a sudden burst of deafening applause, and out through the passage, the Emperor watching them in breathless astonishment until they disappear, when he rushes from his box and descends the steps in frantic excitement.

ANDROCLES AND THE LION

THE EMPEROR. My friends, an incredible! an amazing thing! has happened. I can no longer doubt the truth of Christianity. [*The Christians press to him joyfully*]. This Christian sorcerer— [*with a yell, he breaks off as he sees Androcles and the lion emerge from the passage, waltzing. He bolts wildly up the steps into his box, and slams the door. All, Christians and gladiators alike, fly for their lives, the gladiators bolting into the arena, the others in all directions. The place is emptied with magical suddenness*].

ANDROCLES [*naïvely*] Now I wonder why they all run away from us like that. [*The lion, combining a series of yawns, purrs, and roars, achieves something very like a laugh*].

THE EMPEROR [*standing on a chair inside his box and looking over the wall*] Sorcerer: I command you to put that lion to death instantly. It is guilty of high treason. Your conduct is most disgra—[*the lion charges at him up the stairs*] help! [*He disappears. The lion rears against the box; looks over the partition at him; and roars. The Emperor darts out through the door and down to Androcles, pursued by the lion*].

ANDROCLES. Dont run away, sir: he cant help springing if you run. [*He seizes the Emperor and gets between him and the lion, who stops at once*]. Dont be afraid of him.

THE EMPEROR. I am not afraid of him. [*The lion crouches, growling. The Emperor clutches Androcles*]. Keep between us.

ANDROCLES. Never be afraid of animals, your worship: thats the great secret. He'll be as gentle as a lamb when he knows that you are his friend. Stand quite still; and smile; and let him smell you all over just to reassure him; for, you see, he's afraid of you; and he must examine you thoroughly before he gives you his confidence. [*To the lion*] Come now, Tommy; and speak nicely to the Emperor, the great good Emperor who has power to have all our heads cut off if we dont behave very very respectfully to him.

The lion utters a fearful roar. The Emperor dashes madly up the steps, across the landing, and down again on the other side, with the lion in hot pursuit. Androcles rushes after the lion; overtakes him as he is descending; and throws himself on his back, trying to use his toes as a brake. Before he can stop him the lion gets hold of the trailing end of the Emperor's robe.

ANDROCLES. Oh bad wicked Tommy, to chase the Emperor like that! Let go the Emperor's robe at once, sir: wheres your manners? [*The lion growls and worries the robe*]. Dont pull it away from him, your worship. He's only playing. Now I shall be really angry with you, Tommy, if you dont let go. [*The lion growls again*]. I'll tell you what it is, sir: he thinks you and I are not friends.

THE EMPEROR [*trying to undo the clasp of his brooch*] Friends! You infernal scoundrel [*the lion growls*]—dont let him go. Curse this brooch! I cant get it loose.

ANDROCLES. We mustnt let him lash himself into a rage. You must shew him that you are my particular friend—if you will have the condescension. [*He seizes the Emperor's hands and shakes them cordially*]. Look, Tommy: the nice Emperor is the dearest friend Andy Wandy has in the whole world: he loves him like a brother.

THE EMPEROR. You little brute, you damned filthy little dog of a Greek tailor: I'll have you burnt alive for daring to touch the divine person of the Emperor. [*The lion growls*].

ANDROCLES. Oh dont talk like that, sir. He understands every word you say: all animals do: they take it from the tone of your voice. [*The lion growls and lashes his tail*]. I think he's going to spring at your worship. If you wouldnt mind saying something affectionate. [*The lion roars*].

THE EMPEROR [*shaking Androcles's hand frantically*] My dearest Mr Androcles, my sweetest friend, my long lost brother, come to my arms. [*He embraces Androcles*]. Oh, what an abominable smell of garlic!

The lion lets go the robe and rolls over on his back, clasping his forepaws over one another coquettishly above his nose.

ANDROCLES. There! You see, your worship, a child might play with him now. See! [*He tickles the lion's belly. The lion wriggles ecstatically*]. Come and pet him.

THE EMPEROR. I must conquer these unkingly terrors. Mind you dont go away from him, though. [*He pats the lion's chest*].

ANDROCLES. Oh, sir, how few men would have the courage to do that!

THE EMPEROR. Yes: it takes a bit of nerve. Let us have the Court in and frighten them. Is he safe, do you think?

ANDROCLES. Quite safe now, sir.

THE EMPEROR [*majestically*] What ho, there! All who are within hearing, return without fear. Caesar has tamed the lion. [*All the fugitives steal cautiously in. The menagerie keeper comes from the passage with other keepers armed with iron bars and tridents*]. Take those things away. I have subdued the beast. [*He places his foot on it*].

FERROVIUS [*timidly approaching the Emperor and looking down with awe on the lion*] It is strange that I, who fear no man, should fear a lion.

THE CAPTAIN. Every man fears something, Ferrovius.

THE EMPEROR. How about the Pretorian Guard now?

FERROVIUS. In my youth I worshipped Mars, the God of War. I turned from him to serve the Christian god; but today the Christian god forsook me; and Mars overcame me and took back his own. The Christian god is not yet. He will come when Mars and I are dust; but meanwhile I must serve the gods that are, not the God that will be. Until then I accept service in the Guard, Caesar.

THE EMPEROR. Very wisely said. All really sensible men agree that the prudent course is to be neither bigoted in our attachment to the old nor rash and unpractical in keeping an open mind for the new, but to make the best of both dispensations.

THE CAPTAIN. What do you say, Lavinia? Will you too be prudent?

LAVINIA [*on the stairs*] No: I'll strive for the coming of the God who is not yet.

THE CAPTAIN. May I come and argue with you occasionally?

LAVINIA. Yes, handsome Captain: you may. [*He kisses her hand*].

THE EMPEROR. And now, my friends, though I do not, as you see, fear this lion, yet the strain of his presence is considerable; for none of us can feel quite sure what he will do next.

THE MENAGERIE KEEPER. Caesar: give us this Greek sorcerer to be a slave in the menagerie. He has a way with the beasts.

ANDROCLES [distressed] Not if they are in cages. They should not be kept in cages. They must be all let out.

THE EMPEROR. I give this sorcerer to be a slave to the first man who lays hands on him. [The menagerie keepers and the gladiators rush for Androcles. The lion starts up and faces them. They surge back]. You see how magnanimous we Romans are, Androcles. We suffer you to go in peace.

ANDROCLES. I thank your worship. I thank you all, ladies and gentlemen. Come, Tommy. Whilst we stand together, no cage for you: no slavery for me. [He goes out with the lion, everybody crowding away to give him as wide a berth as possible].

Afterword

In this play I have presented one of the Roman persecutions of the early Christians, not as the conflict of a false theology with a true, but as what all such persecutions essentially are: an attempt to suppress a propaganda that seemed to threaten the interests involved in the established law and order, organized and maintained in the name of religion and justice by politicians who are pure opportunist Have-and-Holders. People who are shewn by their inner light the possibility of a better world based on the demand of the spirit for a nobler and more abundant life, not for themselves at the expense of others, but for everybody, are naturally dreaded and therefore hated by the Have-and-Holders, who keep always in reserve two sure weapons against them. The first is a persecution effected by the provocation, organization, and arming of that herd instinct which makes men abhor all departures from custom, and, by the most cruel punishments and the wildest calumnies, force eccentric people to behave and profess exactly as other people do. The second is by leading the herd to war, which immediately and infallibly makes them forget everything, even their most cherished and hardwon public liberties and private interests, in the irresistible surge of their pugnacity and the tense preoccupation of their terror.

There is no reason to believe that there was anything more in the Roman persecutions than this. The attitude of the Roman Emperor and the officers of his staff towards the opinions at issue were much the same as those of a modern British Home Secretary towards members of the lower middle classes when some pious policeman charges them with Bad Taste, technically called blasphemy: Bad Taste being a violation of Good Taste, which in such matters practically means Hypocrisy. The Home Secretary and the judges who try the case are usually far more sceptical and blasphemous than the poor men whom they persecute; and their professions of horror at the blunt utterance of their own opinions are revolting to those behind the scenes who have any genuine religious sensibility; but the thing is done because the governing classes, provided only the law against blasphemy is not applied to themselves, strongly approve of such persecution because it enables them to represent their own privileges as part of the religion of the country.

Therefore my martyrs are the martyrs of all time, and my persecutors the persecutors of all time. My Emperor, who has no sense of the value of common people's lives, and amuses himself with killing as carelessly as with sparing, is the sort of monster you can make of any silly-clever-gentleman by idolizing him. We are still so easily imposed on by such idols that one of the leading pastors of the Free Churches in London denounced my play on the ground that my persecuting Emperor is a very fine fellow, and the persecuted Christians ridiculous. From which I conclude that a popular pulpit may be as perilous to a man's soul as an imperial throne.

All my articulate Christians, the reader will notice, have different enthusiasms, which they accept as the same religion only because it involves them in a common opposition to the official religion and consequently in a common doom. Androcles is a humanitarian naturalist, whose views surprise everybody. Lavinia, a clever and fearless freethinker, shocks the Pauline Ferrovius, who is comparatively stupid and conscience ridden. Spintho, the blackguardly debauchee, is presented as one of the typical Christians of that period on the authority of St Augustine, who seems to have come to the conclusion at one period of his development that most Christians were what we call wrong uns. No doubt he was to some extent right: I have had occasion often to point out that revolutionary movements attract those who are not good enough for established institutions as well as those who are too good for them.

But the most striking aspect of the play at this moment is the terrible topicality given it by the war. We were at peace when I pointed out, by the mouth of Ferrovius, the path of an honest man who finds out, when the trumpet sounds, that he cannot follow Jesus. Many years earlier, in The Devil's Disciple, I touched the same theme even more definitely, and shewed the minister throwing off his black coat for ever when he discovered, amid the thunder of the captains and the shouting, that he was a born fighter. Great numbers of our clergy have found themselves of late in the position of Ferrovius and Anthony Anderson. They have discovered that they hate not only their enemies but everyone who does not share their hatred, and that they want to fight and to force other people to fight. They have turned their churches into recruiting stations and their vestries into munition workshops. But it has never occurred to them to take off their black coats and say quite simply, "I find in the hour of trial that the Sermon on the Mount is tosh, and that I am not a Christian. I apologize for all the unpatriotic nonsense I have been preaching all these years. Have the goodness to give me a revolver and a commission in a regiment which has for its chaplain a priest of the god Mars: *my* God." Not a bit of it. They have stuck to their livings and served Mars in the name of Christ, to the scandal of all religious mankind. When the Archbishop of York behaved like a gentleman and the Head Master of Eton preached a Christian sermon, and were reviled by the rabble, the Martian parsons encouraged the rabble. For this they made no apologies or excuses, good or bad. They simply indulged their passions, just as they had always indulged their class prejudices and commercial interests, without troubling themselves for a moment as to whether they were Christians or not. They did not protest even when a body calling itself the Anti-German League (not having noticed, apparently, that it had been anticipated by the British Empire, the French Republic, and the Kingdoms of Italy, Japan, and Serbia) actually succeeded in closing a church at Forest Hill in which God was worshipped in the German language. One would have supposed that this grotesque outrage on the commonest decencies of religion would have provoked a remonstrance from even the worldliest bench of bishops. But no: apparently it seemed to the bishops as natural that the House of God should be looted when He allowed German to be spoken in it as that a baker's shop with a German name over the door should be pillaged. Their verdict was, in effect, "Serve God right, for creating the Germans!" The incident would have been impossible in a country where the Church was as powerful as the Church of England, had it had at the same time a spark of catholic as distinguished from tribal religion in it. As it is, the thing occurred; and as far as I have observed, the only people who gasped were the Freethinkers.

Thus we see that even among men who make a profession of religion the great majority are as Martian as the majority of their congregations. The average clergyman is an official who makes his living by christening babies, marrying adults, conducting a ritual, and making the best he can (when he has any conscience about it) of a certain routine of school superintendence, district visiting, and organization of almsgiving, which does not necessarily touch Christianity at any point except the point of the tongue. The exceptional or religious clergyman may be an ardent Pauline salvationist, in which case his more cultivated parishioners dislike him, and say that he ought to have joined the Methodists. Or he may be an artist expressing religious emotion without intellectual definition by means of poetry, music, vestments, and architecture, also producing religious ecstasy by physical expedients, such as fasts and vigils, in which case he is denounced as a Ritualist. Or he may be either a Unitarian Deist like Voltaire or Tom Paine, or the more modern sort of Anglican Theosophist to whom the Holy Ghost is the Élan Vital of Bergson, and the Father and Son are an expression of the fact that our functions and aspects are manifold, and that we are all sons and all either potential or actual parents, in which case he is strongly suspected by the straiter Salvationists of being little better than an Atheist. All these varieties, you see, excite remark. They may be very popular with their congregations; but they are regarded by the average man as the freaks of the Church. The Church, like the society of which it is an organ, is balanced and steadied by the great central Philistine mass above whom theology looms as a highly spoken of and doubtless most important thing, like Greek Tragedy, or classical music, or the higher mathematics, but who are very glad when church is over and they can go home to lunch or dinner, having in fact, for all practical purposes, no reasoned convictions at all, and being equally ready to persecute a poor Freethinker for saying that St James was not infallible, and to send one of the Peculiar People to prison for being so very peculiar as to take St James seriously.

In short, a Christian martyr was thrown to the lions not because he was a Christian, but because he was a crank: that is, an unusual sort of person. And multitudes of people, quite as civilized and amiable as we, crowded to see the lions eat him just as they now crowd the lion-house in the Zoo at feeding-time, not because they really cared twopence about Diana or Christ, or could have given you any intelligent or correct account of the things Diana and Christ stood against one another for, but simply because they wanted to see a curious and exciting spectacle. You, dear reader, have probably run to see a fire; and if somebody came in now and told you that a lion was chasing a man down the street you would rush to the window. And if anyone were to say that you were as cruel as the people who let the lion loose on the man, you would be justly indignant. Now that we may no longer see a man hanged, we assemble outside the jail to see the black flag run up. That is our duller method of enjoying ourselves in the old Roman spirit. And if the Government decided to throw persons of unpopular or eccentric views to the lions in the Albert Hall or the Earl's Court stadium tomorrow, can you doubt that all the seats would be crammed, mostly by people who could not give you the most superficial account of the views in question. Much less unlikely things have happened. It is true that if such a revival does take place soon, the martyrs will not be members of heretical religious sects: they will be Peculiars, Anti-Vivisectionists, Flat-Earth men, scoffers at the laboratories, or infidels who refuse to kneel down when a procession of doctors goes by. But the lions will hurt them just as much, and the spectators will enjoy themselves just as much, as the Roman lions and spectators used to do.

It was currently reported in the Berlin newspapers that when Androcles was first performed in Berlin, the Crown Prince rose and left the house, unable to endure the (I hope) very clear and fair exposition of autocratic Imperialism given by the Roman captain to his Christian prisoners. No English Imperialist was intelligent and earnest enough to do the same in London. If the report is correct, I confirm the logic of the Crown Prince, and am glad to find myself so well understood. But I can assure him that the Empire which served for my model when I wrote Androcles was, as he is now finding to his cost, much nearer my home than the German one.

Notes

The notes in this edition are intended to serve the needs of overseas students as well as those of British-born users.

Inverted commas indicate references to stage directions.

Prologue

107 *'Prologue':* a formal introduction. This is a standard dramatic device used, as in this case, to give the audience important information about events that took place before the main action of Acts I and II. Without this information the final scenes of Act II would not make sense.

'Overture': usually a musical term for an orchestral piece that opens an opera and contains references to all the main musical themes to be heard later. Here it refers to the off-stage sounds which Shaw has orchestrated to introduce Christians and lions, both central to the future action. This is a subtle use of sound to create a mood and give information at the same time.

'Megaera': the name suggests that Androcles's wife is not very pleasant for it is also the name of one of the Furies of classical Greek literature.

'pampered': over indulged, made too much fuss of.

'prime of life': when health and strength are at their best.

108 *laughing-stock:* someone who is made fun of, mocked, usually in public.

shrew: sharp-tongued woman.

butter wouldnt melt in your mouth: a saying meaning that someone is gentle in manner and voice. Implies a false show of innocence.

109 *blaspheming:* speaking offensively about God and religion.

156

atheists: people who do not believe in the existence of any God or gods.

public-house: place where alcoholic drinks are sold. An example of Shaw modernizing the language of his characters to make it instantly recognizable.

addicted: unable to stop.

cur: dog.

stout: too large or fat.

dont take on: don't upset yourself.

110 *Andy:* shortened version of Androcles with a modern ring.

'*totters*': walks unsteadily.

Meggy: shortened version of Megaera. See *Andy* above. Suggestion of the two as a music-hall pair.

pretty nigh: almost, nearly.

'*quaking*': trembling.

111 *tootsums wootsums:* baby language meaning 'foot' or 'toes'. Androcles speaks like a mother to her young child when talking to the lion.

velvet paws: an expression meaning 'keep your claws in'.

'*waltz*': a ballroom dance invented in the nineteenth century and still popular today.

Act I

113 '*converging*': the roads meet at this point.

'*triumphal arches*': the Romans built magnificent arches to celebrate the growth of their Empire.

'*debouch*': come together in an open space.

'*centurion*': officer in charge of a company of a hundred men.

'*cudgel*': heavy stick carried to indicate his authority.

'*dogged*': resolute.

'*cohort*': troop of Roman soldiers.

Captain: There were no captains in the Roman Army. An example of Shaw ignoring historical details. It has the advantage that the audience may easily identify his rank and social position, and brings the play closer to us.

larks: tricks or games.

Coliseum: large amphitheatre in Ancient Rome. Many Christians were killed there during the persecutions. A large part of the Coliseum remains in ruins today.

gladiators: men trained to fight each other for sport in Ancient Rome. Sometimes they fought wild beasts or Christians.

'patrician': a nobleman.

114 *profanity:* not religious or heathen. Here it is blasphemy against Roman orthodoxy. Throughout the Romans treat Christianity as if it were not a religion.

Onward Christian Soldiers: another modernization or anachronism. This is a famous nineteenth-century hymn, still popular today.

115 *inadmissable:* not allowable.

abhorrence: hatred and disgust.

Imperial Circus ... Imperial Menagerie: the Emperor's company of gladiators and wild beasts used to entertain at the Coliseum. Many Christians died, often without defending themselves.

persecution: deliberate attack with the intention of causing harm. Especially, as in this case, where religious beliefs are concerned.

'sardonic': mocking.

Defender of the Faith: a modernization. This title was granted to Henry VIII in 1521 by the Pope when Henry was attacking Protestants. Henry turned against the Pope when he was not allowed to divorce his wife but he and all subsequent British monarchs still kept the title. By using this term Shaw makes a parallel between Rome and Britain.

116 *divine personage:* Roman emperors thought of themselves as gods. This idea is common with rulers and kings. In England and other parts of Europe 'the divine right of kings' meant that the king was inspired through God in his

decisions. In addition the right of rule itself was sacrosanct and it was a sin to challenge it as it came direct from God. It was successfully challenged with the execution of Charles I in the seventeenth century.

imputation: accusation.

sacrilege: sin against a holy person or object.

incense: sweet smelling spice burned in honour of the gods. It was one of the gifts of the Three Wise Men to the infant Jesus and is still used in churches.

clemency: mercy.

suicide: the taking of one's own life.

martyr: a person who dies for his or her beliefs.

117 *'titter':* giggle.

legion: the Roman Army was divided into units of 3000–6000 men.

armorer: maker of weapons and armour.

sorcerer: magician.

receipt: written acceptance of delivery.

countersigned: signed in agreement by the other party.

'nap': short rest or sleep.

118 *'humane':* kind, gentle.

flirting: playing, laughing, in an amorous way.

Incorrigible: incurable: beyond correction.

voluptuaries: people who are obsessed with sensual gratification usually in a perverse form, such as the Captain goes on to describe.

rabble: mob, unruly crowd.

riff-raff: unimportant, unruly hangers-on.

Jupiter: the chief of the Roman gods. Zeus is the Greek name.

Diana: a Roman goddess, a virgin and a huntress.

119 *symbol:* a thing that through tradition or general agreement stands for another thing or things. Here the 'iron statue' represents an image of 'terror and darkness' to Lavinia.

Pray God .: . false pride: though Christians may be proud of their religion they must in all other matters be humble.

False pride is vanity.

120 *no future beyond the grave:* the Captain denies the Christian heaven.

'*retinue*': train of followers.

'*courtiers*': members of the Emperor's court.

'*epicene*': somewhat feminine in appearance.

Jove: another name for Jupiter.

chaff: tease or mock.

121 *turn the other cheek:* Christians are not allowed to resist bad treatment actively. Jesus is reported to have said: 'You have heard that it was said, "An eye for an eye, and a tooth for a tooth." But I say to you, Do not resist one who is evil. But if any one strikes you on the right cheek, turn to him the other also ... You have heard that it was said, "You shall love your neighbour and hate your enemy." But I say to you, Love your enemies and pray for those who persecute you, so that you may be sons of your Father who is in heaven.' (St Matthew's Gospel, 5: 38–45). These instructions can be seen as the chief explanation for the Christians allowing themselves to be thrown to the lions without resistance. Much of the dramatic action centres on the capacity of the central characters to obey this code of behaviour.

cad: not a true gentleman. A common Edwardian term.

Pull yourself together: behave yourself.

Plucky little filly!: expression meaning, literally, 'brave young female horse'. Lentulus is impressed with Lavinia's spirit. The phrase is slang, reminiscent of the race course and of the upper-middle classes.

'*choleric*': bad tempered.

'*debauchee*': person who is morally weak and who leads a bad life.

'*convulsively*': with difficulty.

122 *Billy goat:* male goat.

mobs: attacks with others.

Revile me: curse and swear at me.

piety: respect for God and Man.

123 *'out of countenance':* embarrassed, made to look foolish.

'paternal': fatherly.

trifle: small amount.

square: pay him back.

124 *Cappadocia:* now part of Turkey.

white as snow: the shock was too much. It is a popular belief that shock can turn hair white.

overwrought: overcome, very tense.

125 *'unction':* fervour.

backslidings: failures, falling away from the path of Christian behaviour.

infidels: unbelievers.

126 *'meditation':* deep thought.

Peter: Ferrovius refers to St Peter, one of the twelve Apostles. On the night Jesus was arrested Peter denied that he knew Jesus on three separate occasions.

blackguard: villain, criminal.

crack in the gate: Heaven is popularly imagined as having gates: St Peter has the keys.

scores: debts.

127 *plague:* fatal illness often thought to have been sent by God as punishment for evil.

128 *souls:* orthodox Christians believe that only humans have souls and thus animals cannot go to heaven.

Tention!: attention.

trot along spry: move on quickly and smartly.

'goad': spiked stick.

129 *emetic:* substance that causes vomiting.

'the lion': the audience would see that it is Androcles's pantomime lion.

Act II

130 *'eyes blazing':* wild with anger.

'trident': weapon with three prongs.

'visor': front part of the helmet that may be raised and lowered.

'editor': manages the gladiators and the Christians.

'Call Boy': Person who summons the performers.

turn down their thumbs: the audience would turn down their thumbs to show that the loser should be killed, or up to indicate that he should be spared.

talents: a talent was a large amount of money.

131 *vestal virgins*: priestesses of the goddess Vesta.

he likes animals: there are many stories of Jupiter turning himself into an animal to seduce human females.

132 *disoblige*: refuse.

Dog of an apostate: traitor of religious faith, vows or principles.

Iscariot: Judas Iscariot: the man who betrayed Jesus to the Jews. Also one of the twelve Apostles.

Get thee behind him, Satan: don't tempt him to do wrong. Satan is a name for the devil.

For two pins: for next to nothing.

134 *before you could say Balbus*: very quickly. Absurd equivalent of 'before you could say Jack Robinson'.

bitters: alcoholic liquor supposed to increase appetite.

'bolts precipitately': runs away very quickly before the Emperor sees him.

'suite': attendants and followers.

those about to die salute thee: believed to be the traditional salute of the gladiators.

'bluff respect': the Editor shows Metellus that he thinks himself just as good as he is.

135 *walking conscience*: always commenting on how others ought to behave.

136 *Pretorian Guard*: personal bodyguard of the Emperor.

Archangels: the chief angels, God's special messengers.

'Obsequious': servile, dutiful.

sesterces: small coins of little value.

137 *my Master's will*: what Jesus wished.

138 *sweet-by-and-by:* in Heaven. Expression from sentimental late Victorian hymn: 'In the sweet by-and-by/We shall meet on that beautiful shore ...'.

139 *lamb to the slaughter:* Jesus was seen as a lamb – innocent and gentle. Also a reference to Christians as sheep and Christ as their shepherd is intended.

   ram: male sheep.

140 *That passage ... to Calvary:* Jesus was killed on a hill called Calvary.

141 *'sardonically':* bitterly and cynically. His feelings are mixed.

142 *hauled down the flag:* expression meaning surrender, usually in battle when the losers lower their flag to indicate that they have lost.

143 *'Etruscan':* Etruscans were the Ancient people of central Italy.

   'clamor': noise.

144 *Domitian:* Roman Emperor, AD 81–96.

   Gaul: native of the area which is now France.

146 *'He marches out along the passage':* this following section requires a scene change. The original production used a revolving stage. The stage returns to the previous setting at the end of the page, when the Emperor rushes from his box.

   'portcullis': gate that may be raised or lowered.

148 *'coquettishly':* playfully flirtatious.

149 *Mars:* the Roman god of war.

   prudent: discreet, worldly-wise.

   bigoted: prejudiced.

   dispensations: systems of order.

150 *magnanimous:* generous.

Study questions

Prologue

1 Imagine that you are Megaera and
   (a) describe what you think it is like to be married to
   Androcles with special reference to his Christianity and to
   his love of animals;
   (b) say how you would like him to behave.
2 Much of the action that takes place in the Prologue is written
   in the stage directions. Write your own account of these
   events.
3 Describe, with examples, two different kinds of humour that
   Shaw uses here.

Act I

4 Shaw presents several characters who express different
   attitudes towards religion:
   (a) compare those of the Captain and Lavinia;
   (b) compare those of Ferrovius and Androcles;
   (c) describe Spintho's view.
5 'So thats how you convert, brother.' Describe Ferrovius's
   method of conversion as demonstrated by the scene with
   Lentulus, and say what you think of it.
6 Ferrovius lacks a sense of humour. Show how Shaw exploits
   this both to make the audience laugh and to convey an
   impression of Ferrovius's character.
7 Take Lavinia's speech beginning: 'That is the strange thing,
   Captain' until 'I tell you, it is physically impossible' (pages
   118–19). Read it aloud and then
   (a) say how the style differs from everyday speech, showing
   how Shaw emphasizes what is being said;